AQA GCSE

English

Skills for Achieving an A*

Philip Allan Updates, an imprint of Hodder Education, an Hachette UK company, Market Place, Deddington, Oxfordshire OX15 0SE

Orders

Bookpoint Ltd, 130 Milton Park, Abingdon, Oxfordshire OX14 4SB
tel: 01235 827720
fax: 01235 400454
e-mail: uk.orders@bookpoint.co.uk

Lines are open 9.00 a.m.–5.00 p.m., Monday to Saturday, with a 24-hour message answering service.

You can also order through the Philip Allan Updates website:
www.philipallan.co.uk

© Philip Allan Updates 2010
ISBN 978-1-4441-1081-4

First printed 2010
Impression number 5 4 3 2 1
Year 2015   2014   2013   2012   2011   2010

Printed in Italy

Hachette UK's policy is to use papers that are natural, renewable and recyclable products and made from wood grown in sustainable forests. The logging and manufacturing processes are expected to conform to the environmental regulations of the country of origin.

P01742

Contents

Introduction

There are not many GCSE English textbooks on the market which focus solely on A* skills, so why do A* students need this kind of book? Well, the main reason is that most English Departments across the country are rightly focusing on gaining as many C grade passes as possible in their schools. That leaves the 5% of potential A* candidates with little or no idea of how to attain their aim.

First, 5% of students translates to round about 10 A* students per school, so this book has to be interesting enough for you to be able to follow the course independently. The authors are highly experienced teachers and examiners who have many years of experience in different schools. We have pooled our experience to make sure we give you something engaging and refreshingly different to study in small groups.

Second, this book provides a different way of approaching GCSE English by focusing on the Assessment Objectives upon which the AQA GCSE English course is based. It is a skills-based course book which recognises the fact that there is little or no content in English and English Literature.

However, because this book is based on Assessment Objectives, it can be used for any examination board. The AOs in speaking and listening, reading and writing are the same for every board, so students and teachers can use this book whatever summative assessment they are aiming for. This book equips students with the skills to gain an A* and is not tied to specific examinations or controlled conditions tasks. Teachers may wish to focus on one discrete component, like reading poetry, or integrate aspects from each section, especially the use of speaking and listening as a fundamental means for students to arrive at their own meanings and to learn, rather than be taught.

Third, the integral use of examiner comments on sample student work gives you an unprecedented view into the mind of an examiner. This will not only help you to make sense of the world of examining and assessment, but will also allow you to assess yourselves (known as Assessment for Learning in modern educational parlance) and to see the clear links between one grade and the next.

Finally, this book is different from other textbooks in terms of its structure. It focuses on the English Language/English Literature route in the AQA specification which most A* students will be following. The first section covers reading as a portable skill, which reinforces the links between the reading and writing Assessment Objectives wherever they may be assessed. You must find evidence to back up your explanations in controlled conditions work and the exam papers, so it makes sense to focus on the portable skill rather than the content.

The next two pages show you the special features of this book and how to use them. So, get started and see what it takes to gain an A*!

John Nield
Graham Fletcher
Unsah Tabassum

Also available from the same authors:

AQA GCSE English: Skills for Language & Literature
(978-1-4441-0874-3)

A textbook which allows students to develop their reading, writing, speaking and listening skills to achieve best results in their exams and controlled assessment.

AQA GCSE English: Skills for Language & Literature Teacher Guide + CD
(978-1-4441-0875-0)

Included within this guide is a CD-ROM with all the audio material to support the speaking and listening activities in the *Skills for Language & Literature* textbook. The Teacher Guide also contains: skills teaching map, activities with teacher notes, worksheets and answers, photocopiable planning grids, assessment advice and PowerPoints.

How to use this book

Tasks: these are provided throughout the book to encourage you to apply the skills you need in order to do well.

Highlighting: coloured highlighting links the examiner's comments to the student responses, showing what is required to gain marks.

Student responses: sample answers to the set tasks.

Section B   Speaking and listening

Assessment Objectives for speaking and listening

5

Task A

Read the extract below, which comes from an interview for a headteacher's post. It is the candidate's response to the question, 'What is your vision for the school?'

Give a talk to the rest of your class explaining the changes you would make to your school if you were headteacher.

'Change? Who needs it? I have examined this school in detail and my considered opinion is that you do. Need change, I mean.

'Why? I believe that schools are for the students. It is the students who should be at the heart of all of our important decisions. Not only that, they should be involved in making those decisions. It would be my intention, if appointed as headteacher, to consult widely with students about what they consider to be the strengths and weaknesses of the school.

'Having been round the school this morning, it is clear that its fabric is in a deteriorating condition. The amount of litter is intolerable and the state of the toilets is a disgrace, bordering on a health hazard. I believe these should be priorities for financial investment. I expect the highest possible standards from our students. How can we expect them to perform highly and respect their environment if we do not give them the best?

'The range of subjects we offer our students is too narrow. Lessons should encourage students to participate, to enjoy and to achieve. We need to design an experience that is exciting and relevant for all of our students. I envisage far-reaching reforms for the curriculum. Diplomas would be central to our planning. I want children to want to come to this school so I would offer them exciting events both in and outside school, refreshing approaches to teaching, and the opportunity to develop to their maximum potential.'

Student response to Task A

What's it like to play at being God? Some people think that's what headteachers do. They control the lives of hundreds of people. If they get it right everyone benefits. If they get it wrong…

I don't intend to get it wrong. A headteacher's job is all about making choices. To do that, they need information. My choices will be made using the best possible information — my experience. I know this school in detail. I know the places the bullies haunt like gruesome ghouls. I know how horrible school meals are. I know how uncomfortable the uniform is. I will do a fantastic job because, as my mother says, like every teenager, I know it all!

Doubtless you think you could do just as well. Let's face it: we are all experts on education. We have been immersed in it since our early years. That means you'll be able to appreciate the complexity of the job I'm going to do. Lessons, buildings, uniform… They all need attention. In fact, some of them need a magic wand.

So what's my motivation for all this? It isn't to play God. It's to make life better for everyone, and if I do that I'll benefit as much as anyone else. Unfortunately I'm not Harry Potter. I need you to work with me. Just consider our potential. Some people try to *use* magic. Together we can *be* magic.

Examiner's comment

The speaker's main ideas are cogently expressed, using standard English and a varied vocabulary. There are clear attempts to connect with the audience through the opening question and use of the word 'you'. The rhetorical questions force the audience members to consider their own opinions. Irony is used effectively.

Although the speaker makes a series of points, none of them are expanded fully. The thinking behind the ideas is explained clearly, but the candidate has not actually identified the changes to be made. Nevertheless, this answer would fulfil most of the Grade A descriptors.

How to improve

To achieve a Grade A*, the candidate needs to develop some of the points more and attempt to create a more inventive organisation of the material.

Assessment for learning

Read the third paragraph again. Identify opportunities for the student to expand upon the points being made. Discuss your findings with a partner and rewrite the paragraph.

Task B

Write a response to Task A that will get you at least a Grade A.

Remember: there are three parts to this activity: the opening, your ideas and explanations, and the ending. They are all important.

How to improve: advice from the examiner on how student responses could be improved to achieve more marks.

Assessment for Learning: activities that allow students to practise their skills in solo and group work.

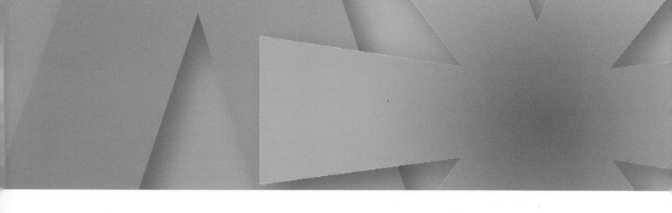

Examiner's comments: these highlight the good and bad points of student responses.

Remember boxes: these are used throughout the book to remind you of exactly what the examiners are looking for.

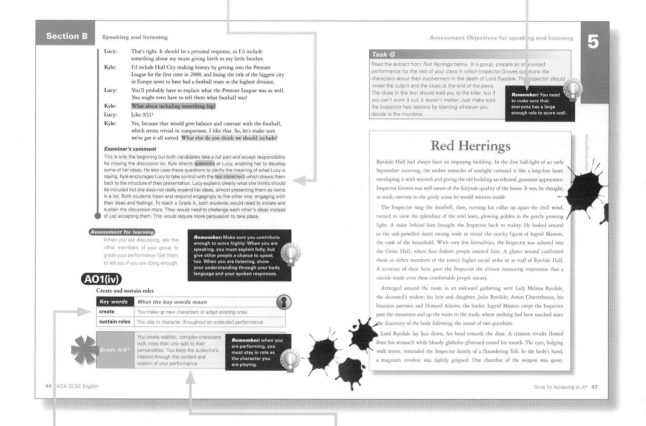

The book spread shown contains:

Section B — Speaking and listening

Lucy: That's right. It should be a personal response, so I'd include something about my mum giving birth to my little brother.

Kyle: I'd include Hull City making history by getting into the Premier League for the first time in 2008, and losing the title of the biggest city in Europe never to have had a football team in the highest division.

Lucy: You'll probably have to explain what the Premier League was as well. You might even have to tell them what football was!

Kyle: What about including something big?

Lucy: Like 9/11?

Kyle: Yes, because that would give balance and contrast with the football, which seems trivial in comparison. I like that. So, let's make sure we've got it all sorted. What else do you think we should include?

Examiner's comment

This is only the beginning but both candidates take a full part and accept responsibility for moving the discussion on. Kyle directs questions at Lucy, enabling her to develop some of her ideas. He also uses these questions to clarify the meaning of what Lucy is saying. Kyle encourages Lucy to take control with the last statement which draws them back to the structure of their presentation. Lucy explains clearly what she thinks should be included but she does not really expand her ideas, almost presenting them as items in a list. Both students listen and respond engagingly to the other one, engaging with their ideas and feelings. To reach a Grade A, both students would need to initiate and sustain the discussion more. They would need to challenge each other's ideas instead of just accepting them. This would require more persuasion to take place.

Assessment for learning

When you are discussing, ask the other members of your group to grade your performance. Get them to tell you if you are doing enough.

Remember: Make sure you contribute enough to score highly! When you are speaking, you must explain fully, but give other people a chance to speak too. When you are listening, show your understanding through your body language and your spoken responses.

AO1(iv)

Create and sustain roles

Key words	What the key words mean
create	You make up new characters or adapt existing ones.
sustain roles	You stay in character throughout an extended performance.

Grade A/A* You create realistic, complex characters with more than one side to their personalities. You keep the audience's interest through the content and realism of your performance.

Remember: when you are performing, you must stay in role as the character you are playing.

46 AQA GCSE English

Task G

Read the extract from *Red Herrings* below. In a group, prepare an improvised performance for the rest of your class in which Inspector Groves questions the characters about their involvement in the death of Lord Ryedale. The Inspector should reveal the culprit and the clues at the end of the piece. The clues in the text should lead you to the killer, but if you can't work it out, it doesn't matter. Just make sure the Inspector has reasons for blaming whoever you decide is the murderer.

Remember: You need to make sure that everyone has a large enough role to score well.

Red Herrings

Ryedale Hall had always been an imposing building. In the dim half-light of an early September morning, the amber tentacles of sunlight caressed it like a long-lost lover, enveloping it with warmth and giving the old building an ethereal, gossamer appearance. Inspector Groves was well aware of the fairytale quality of the house. It was, he thought, in stark contrast to the grisly scene he would witness inside.

The Inspector rang the doorbell, then, turning his collar up again the chill wind, turned to view the splendour of the oval lawn, glowing golden in the gently growing light. A noise behind him brought the Inspector back to reality. He looked around as the oak-panelled doors swung wide to reveal the stocky figure of Ingrid Masters, the cook of the household. With very few formalities, the Inspector was ushered into the Great Hall, where four forlorn people awaited him. A glance around confirmed them as either members of the town's higher social order or as staff of Ryedale Hall. A scrutiny of their faces gave the Inspector the almost reassuring impression that a suicide made even these comfortable people uneasy.

Arranged around the room in an awkward gathering were Lady Melissa Ryedale, the deceased's widow; his heir and daughter, Julia Ryedale; Anton Charterhouse, his business partner; and Howard Adams, the butler. Ingrid Masters swept the Inspector past the mourners and up the stairs to the study, where nothing had been touched since the discovery of the body following the sound of two gunshots.

Lord Ryedale lay face down, his head towards the door. A crimson rivulet flowed from his stomach while bloody globules glistened round his mouth. The eyes, bulging with terror, reminded the Inspector faintly of a floundering fish. In the body's hand, a magnum revolver was tightly gripped. One chamber of the weapon was spent.

Assessment Objectives for speaking and listening — **5**

Skills for Achieving an A* **47**

Key words: a student-friendly decoder of terms used in the Assessment Objectives.

Grade A/A* criteria: these boxes show how the Assessment Objectives are assessed at Grade A/A*.

A

Reading

Chapter 1

Assessment Objectives for reading in English Language

Everyone following the English Language/English Literature route is required to show that they can read with understanding, select appropriate material from different sources and comment on language, presentation and grammar. In addition, you have to develop and sustain a response, and infer (read between the lines). You will not be asked to develop and sustain a response in the externally assessed unit, but you will have to show clear evidence of this skill in controlled assessments.

For English Language, your reading will be marked against the following Assessment Objectives (AOs). The key words and phrases are emboldened and explained in the table overleaf.

AO2(i)	Read and understand texts, selecting material appropriate to purpose, collating different sources and making comparisons and cross-references where appropriate.
AO2(ii)	Develop and sustain interpretations of writers' ideas and perspectives.
AO2(iii)	Explain and evaluate how writers use linguistic, grammatical, structural and presentational features to achieve effects and engage and influence the reader.
AO2(iv)	Understand texts in their social, cultural and historical contexts.

AO2(i)

Read and understand texts, selecting material appropriate to purpose, collating different sources and making comparisons and cross-references where appropriate

Key words	What the key words mean for A* students
read and understand texts	Show understanding of what the writer is aiming to communicate and what he/she may be inferring.
selecting material appropriate to purpose	Choose the relevant references and integrate them within your answer.
collating different sources and making comparisons and cross-references where appropriate	Develop a series of connected comments about two or more texts, finding similarities and differences.

Where is AO2(i) assessed for A*?

This AO is assessed just about every time you are assessed for reading. However, here we are focusing on the reading section (Section A) of Unit 1: understanding and producing non-fiction texts in English Language.

You will be asked to read three different texts in Unit 1 and to answer four different types of question:

(1) retrieval (4 marks)

(2) presentation (8 marks)

(3) inference (8 marks)

(4) comparison/language (16 marks)

How is AO2(i) assessed for A*?

To gain an A* you do not simply need to write more, but you need to show evidence of the following A/A* skills:

1

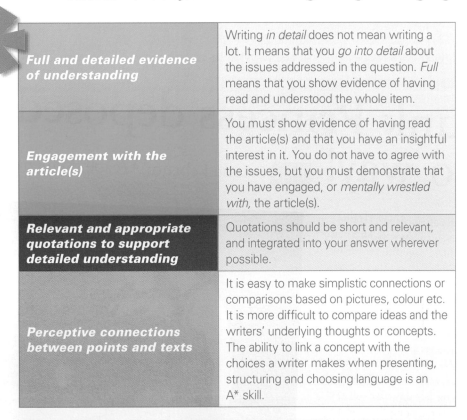

Full and detailed evidence of understanding	Writing *in detail* does not mean writing a lot. It means that you *go into detail* about the issues addressed in the question. *Full* means that you show evidence of having read and understood the whole item.
Engagement with the article(s)	You must show evidence of having read the article(s) and that you have an insightful interest in it. You do not have to agree with the issues, but you must demonstrate that you have engaged, or *mentally wrestled with*, the article(s).
Relevant and appropriate quotations to support detailed understanding	Quotations should be short and relevant, and integrated into your answer wherever possible.
Perceptive connections between points and texts	It is easy to make simplistic connections or comparisons based on pictures, colour etc. It is more difficult to compare ideas and the writers' underlying thoughts or concepts. The ability to link a concept with the choices a writer makes when presenting, structuring and choosing language is an A* skill.

Remember: you have 60 minutes for Section A, which is roughly 90 seconds for each mark. This means, for example, that you should be spending about 24 minutes on Question 4.

Reading and understanding texts

Whether you are following someone else's argument or constructing your own, the way you need to think is similar.

Reading and understanding a text requires the same skills whatever reading task you are doing, be it for controlled or external assessment. You need to ask yourself:

- What is the main point that the writer is making?
- What are the minor points and how do they connect with the main point?
- Does the writer infer any meaning?

This skill is only formally assessed under examination conditions in Unit 1 of your English/English Language course, but you also need to show evidence of it whenever and wherever you read any text-based part of your English course.

Question 1: retrieval

The question on retrieval is worth 4 marks.

Punk Princess deposed? No way!

Pop Sabine Lebrun: Arcade, Manchester

Canadian pop star Sabine Lebrun made headlines last week for a much-publicised bust-up with her parents and management over the lyrics of one of her songs, which allegedly suggested that same-sex relationships were a viable alternative. The song, *Je regrette tous*, was featured in last night's concert and rapturously chanted by her massive teeny-bopper audience, who knew all of the words despite the fact they have only ever appeared on Lebrun's Facebook page.

This is a brave or foolhardy move by Lebrun, whose parents are members of a strict religious sect that bans any reference to same-sex relationships, and they are rumoured to have publicly disowned her at a televised service last Sunday. Neither parent has been willing to talk to the press about what happened, but there has been no secret about Lebrun's antipathy to her parents' beliefs. She included a song entitled *Je ne crois rien* on her last album and this has become an anthem in her anthemically themed set. This is no place for the fainthearted!

Do you remember when Lebrun used to stomp around the set with her guitar and punch the air? Well, she's changed: now she stomps around the stage without her guitar and still punches the air. She is no

Elisanth/Fotolia

Alanis Morissette, but she sure knows how to woo her audience, the average age of which seemed to be 15. No wonder the red-top newspapers are crying 'child protection': this audience is hardly out of nappies!

The negative press reports about her antics and sexual orientation don't seem to bother Sabine as she bounces into her worldwide single success with *Bad Attitude*, which certainly caught this music critic napping. I thought it was the worst sort of 'shriek rock', but what do I know? It got her a Grammy nomination.

In her brisk but purposeful 60-minute set, she invited Sabine look-alikes onto the stage in their pink tights and crimson dyed hair, to strut their stuff in front of this capacity crowd. I was pretty certain that at least two of the invited fans were boys, but hey, Sabine's cool on these things.

Maybe I was wrong about her popularity, but she certainly knows how to play an audience.

Laura Stretton

See more of Sabine Lebrun at the Brighton Hippodrome from tonight until Thursday of this week. Box office open until 7 p.m.

Student response to Task A

Plan

Remember this is a 'what?' question and refer to the whole text.

Success:
- sold a lot of records with *Bad Attitude*
- concert packed out, so still successful
- break-up with parents hints at problems
- her fans still love her

Answer

We learn many things about Lebrun's success and not all that we learn is positive for the pop star. She has certainly been successful because we are told about the success of a former single and the plaudits it brought her. In addition, the writer seems to be surprised that Lebrun is still so successful, as evidenced by the headline.

However, all is not well. Lebrun seems to have had an irrevocable break-up with her parents and her management after a very public argument over some lyrics. This seems to be the only piece of bad news for the pop star, who can fill large venues like the Manchester Arcade with screaming fans who appear to adore her. Lebrun's main success is in her ability to play an audience and she clearly shows that she can still do that.

Examiner's comment

This student focuses clearly on the first three A/A* skills:

- **Full and detailed evidence of understanding:** the answer refers to all of the issues in the article that relate to Sabrine Lebrun's success. The student knows that the other aspects of the article will be addressed in later questions.

- **Engagement with the article:** put another way, this could be described as 'following an argument'. This student obviously understands the subtleties of the text and identifies the main arguments.

- **Relevant and appropriate quotations to support detailed understanding:** examples are highlighted in the text. Note that they are integrated within the text and that there are no direct quotations. This is an A/A* skill.

> **Remember:** you only have about 6 minutes to read the text and write your answer, and you are **not** being assessed for inference. That is required for Question 3 in the examination and Task D in this chapter.

Question 2: presentation

The question on presentation is worth 8 marks.

Task B

Read the following article from a sensationalist tabloid newspaper. How does the presentation of this article add to its effectiveness?

MUSIC

Pink Punk Princess?

Pink-tights-wearing Canadian pop megastar Sa-*has*-bine Lebrun was last night seen luring her immature fans into a pink-panther-like lair with her latest lyrics.

Fans as young as 12 had their ears battered by the Canadian's pink-tinged lyrics about relationships and love.

Isn't it about time that this *has*-bine was banned from our shores? Only last month she was in the news for a big fall-out with her own parents. Now she's trying to break up our British families!

We don't want you in our green and pleasant land, Lebrun, with your pink pouting and punching antics. It's about time you were sent back to where you belong — **French-speaking Canada** – where your lyrics will be better appreciated.

Lebrun? Lepink more like it!

Elisanth/Fotolia

This article is taken from a tabloid newspaper that celebrates celebrities and their misdemeanours. However, it is they who have strayed from even their very low standards of presentation. The amount of pink and emboldened writing is excessive even for this red-top tabloid.

The reporter obviously wishes to criticise Lebrun's latest lyrics without actually saying that they find her attitude to sexuality abhorrent. So they stoop to innuendo by presentation. The overuse of pink ink shows that they believe Lebrun's lyrics to be supportive of single-sex relationships and they do not hold back from suggesting that she goes back home to Canada. And not only to Canada, but French-speaking Canada.

The tabloid has successfully offended two groups in one article: French-Canadians and gays. And how have they done this? By presentation. It is not only the pointedly pink headings and exclamations, but the font size too that helps to amplify their racist rant. You can almost hear the strident voice of its readership screaming their hateful views about Lebrun with words like: 'Now she's trying to break up our British families!' These presentational devices are to the written media what the pub landlord is to comedy: a heavy-handed swipe at whatever it does not understand.

And what can be said about the image? The close proximity of the two band members, the way they are dressed and the guitar slung in a provocative position all fit in with the newspaper's inferences about the sexuality of Lebrun and her band members. Subtle, isn't it?

Examiner's comment

Wherever you are asked to read for assessment purposes, your work is assessed in exactly the same way. A* students are able to link the underlying idea or concept in a text with the devices used by the writer, whether these be presentational or linguistic. In this case, the student has clearly linked the implied meaning of the writer with the presentational devices used, especially when writing about the image.

The student has shown evidence of this skill throughout this entire top-band response. This puts it at A* level.

Remember: this is an examination response and is necessarily short. Your ability to 'develop and sustain' will tend to be shown in controlled conditions assessments.

Task C

Working in a group, choose a presentational device and think of as many ways that it is effective as you can.

Question 3: inference

The question about inference is worth 8 marks.

The dictionary definition of inference is: *'a process of reasoning in which a conclusion is obtained in some way from certain facts, or by hint or implication.'* A more informal definition might be *'reading between the lines'* — or, even more casually, *'nudge, nudge, wink, wink!'*

There is a lot of 'nudging and winking' in the texts from Task B and Task E (opposite). You will only ever be asked to look for inference in one article, so let's practise on the far-from-subtle text from Task B.

Task D

Re-read the text from Task B, 'Pink Punk Princess?' on p. 6. Then copy and complete the following table to explain what you can infer from the quotations. It has already been started for you.

Quotation	Inference
Sa-*has*-bine Lebrun	She is a 'has been' because of her latest lyrics and antics.
pink-tinged lyrics about relationships and love	
We don't want you in our green and pleasant land, Lebrun	
French-speaking Canada	
Lebrun? Lepink, more like it!	There are all sorts of implications and inferences in this quotation, but the overt reference is to…

Sergey Ilin/Fotolia

Sabine Lebrun marries — a man!

We've seen her posing for the cameras with her **girlfriend**. We've read the stories about the **alleged fallout** with her parents. We've even grown used to her shockingly pink hair. But now she's really grabbed the headlines.

Sabine Lebrun has married her childhood sweetheart. **And he's a boy!**

This time around she has shocked us with the very ordinariness of her behaviour. This guy is a skateboarder from Vancouver who likes turkey pizza and Lady GaGa. (We can accept the turkey pizza, but Lady GaGa?!)

Lebrun reportedly spent £1,000 on turkey pizzas for the female fans who had camped outside her house after the recent press campaign about her sexuality.

The wacky singer will have to answer her VERY LOUD FANS who have besieged this newspaper after its recent reports of Lebrun's **alleged affair** with fellow band member, Cherie Passoir.

'We're just good friends,' was the only comment from Lebrun last week, but her fans

Elisanth/Fotolia

will demand a more convincing explanation after her headline-grabbing antics of the past fortnight.

Oh, by the way, her third album is out next week. Strange that, isn't it?

Basically, this newspaper does not like Lebrun. This is inferred in the first paragraph, where there are three examples of the newspaper implying that it is heartily sick of reporting the latest antics of this particular celebrity. The reporter repeats this feeling three times. The article then states her latest antics in detail.

In the following paragraph, the newspaper pretends to be shocked that Lebrun has married a male childhood sweetheart, when it has been party to her renown as a lesbian pop star. The newspaper then implies that he is an ordinary sort of 'guy' who skateboards and dares to be so average as to like turkey pizza and even Lady GaGa: another celebrity pop star who uses the media to her own ends.

This newspaper was obviously party to the media frenzy about Sabine's supposed relationship with a girl band member. It implies that her fans were used in this whole sad affair, despite their having been given a slice of turkey pizza. The final inference is that Lebrun has used the issue of her relationships to court public attention in the run up to the release of her latest album. Perish the thought!

The reader might infer that the newspaper has been a willing participant in the development of this storyline and that there will more to come. Inference and implication are, undoubtedly, the stock in trade of such publications.

Examiner's comments

Section A of Unit 1 assesses reading, but this skill is assessed through your writing. There are no marks directly allocated to writing in this section, but a sophisticated vocabulary and a variety of sentence structures are sure to make a good impression on the examiner (almost by inference!) Writing in an engaging and mature manner will show evidence that you have a 'full and detailed understanding'.

In the response, the higlighted sentences identify:

(1) A short sentence that emphasises effectively the newspaper's duplicity.

(2) Sophisticated and apt vocabulary.

(3) A complex and controlled sentence that adds variety and engages the reader.

(4) Sophisticated and apt vocabulary once more.

(5) A hint of irony to exaggerate the implication/inference.

(6) A concluding sentence that shows a conceptualised view of the whole article and the depth of the student's understanding.

This student shows a perceptive understanding of the inferences and implications in this article. It lacks the detail that would gain the highest mark of 8, but would fall just inside the top band with 7 marks.

(1) Look back at your notes on Task D and develop **three** of the points in the notes.

(2) Exchange your work with another A/A* student and assess each other's work in the same way that the examiner has done for Task E above.

davorr/Fotolia

Develop and sustain interpretations of writers' ideas and perspectives

This AO is mainly addressed under controlled assessment where students have more time to write in detail about specific points — see p. 16.

AO2(iii)

Explain and evaluate how writers use linguistic, grammatical, structural and presentational features to achieve effects and engage and influence the reader

Key words	What the key words mean for A* students
evaluate	to put value on something or to assess how well it works as a device
linguistic	relating to language, but not just words: it means language in its broadest sense and is not about meaning — that is assessed in AO(i)
to achieve effects	why the writer has included this device and what effects the reader believes it has achieved — which may not be what the writer intended
to engage and influence the reader	effects should be included for a reason, and that reason should be to convey the main point, or conceptualisation. A* students should be able to link effects with conceptualisation, so it is key that you meet this AO.

Remember: Higher Tier students will be required to compare language. This is a higher order reading skill.

AO(iii) is assessed in Question 4.

Question 4: comparison/language

There are 16 marks available for the language/comparison question. Because it accounts for 40% of the total reading marks for the reading section, it is worth planning to succeed by:

- comparing like with like
- giving evidence to back up your comparisons
- comparing language, and nothing else

Focus on three or four language points that properly address the question. You will nearly always able to write about:

- the 'person' an article is written in

Valdis Torms/Fotolia

- whether there is any sort of 'semantic field' (a lot of words with the same kind of meaning, or on the same subject)
- the relative formality, or informality, of an article
- whether any linguistic or rhetorical devices have been used (e.g. any rhetorical questions or rules of three; or any use of alliteration)

There are two ways of comparing texts:

(1) Write everything about the use(s) of language in one text. Then include a discourse marker of difference, such as 'however' or 'on the other hand', and write about the use(s) of language in the other item.

(2) Compare each language point as you progress. This allows you to 'focus on comparison throughout the response'.

Task F

Refer to 'Pink Punk Princess?' (p. 6) and *either* 'Punk Princess deposed? No way!' (p. 4) *or* 'Sabine Lebrun marries — a man!' (p. 9). Compare the ways in which language is used for effect in the two texts. Give some examples and explain what the effects are.

Remember: it is always easier, and better, to compare differences rather than continually stating that items are similar. You should therefore think carefully about which two articles to compare. Which has the more different language devices to 'Pink Punk Princess'?

Task G

Look at the following chart. In a group, discuss which of these two articles would be the better to compare with the 'Pink Punk Princess?' article.

'Punk Princess deposed? No way!'	'Sabine Lebrun marries — a man!'
formal	first person
reported speech/third person	relatively informal
French names/titles used a lot	lots of direct addresses to the reader

The better of the two is 'Sabine Lebrun marries — a man!' because of its confrontational attitude towards the celebrity and the greater number of language issues it has to write about. However, drawing comparisons between their relative formality would be tricky.

Two student responses to Task F are set out below. The first student response is an example of the approach to comparison where you write all your points about the first text, add a discourse marker, and then write all your points about the second text.

Student 1 response to Task F

The 'Punk Princess deposed? No Way!' article is from a typical broadsheet newspaper that is trying to appeal to an educated and relatively serious readership with its formal slant on the news. Although there are some informalities like 'teeny bopper' and 'bust-up' (mainly because this sort of concert review would not be aimed at its core readership, who would be relatively old and middle-class), the article is mainly formal in its use of language. This is exemplified by its use of the third person for the most part and by its refusal to infer anything about Lebrun's sexuality. Stretton openly states that there had been rumours about her 'sexual orientation', but refuses to descend into gutter-press innuendo or to be judgemental.

Elisanth/Fotolia

On the other hand, the 'Pink Punk Princess?' article is informal to the point of being offensive. The reporter refers directly to the pop star and to the fact that he believes that she is past it, or a 'has been', by playing on her name. This informality continues in the use of brash capitals and short sentences that exaggerate the point that this is a personalised rant. This relative informality continues into the final sentence, where there is a direct reference to what the paper believes to be Lebrun's inappropriate sexual orientation.

Examiner's comment

This answer is at the top end of the 9–12 mark band and shows clear and relevant evidence that the student has understood the texts. However, to reach the 13–16 mark band and gain an A*, you must show:

- full and detailed understanding
- detailed interpretation and analysis of how the writers use language differently to achieve their effects
- relevant quotations or references
- that you have focused on comparison and cross-referencing between the texts *throughout your response*

Task H

Remind yourself of Task F (on page 12). Then copy and complete the following table.

Language device	'Punk Princess deposed? No way!'	'Sabine Lebrun marries — a man!'
person		
semantic field		
relative formality/ informality		
any linguistic/literary or rhetorical devices used		

The second student response to Task F is an example of comparison where you compare each language point as you progress.

Student 2 response to Task F

'Pink Punk Princess?' is like a slap in the face for the reader as it sets about berating the pop star, Sabine Lebrun. Most of the article is in the third person, as the writer attempts to pour moral scorn on this sinful performer with statements like: 'Now she's trying to break up our British families!' However, the person changes in the next-to-last paragraph where there is a mixture of first ('We don't want') and second ('it's about time you were sent back'), which attempts to engage the reader and to get them to tacitly agree with their increasingly xenophobic and homophobic views.

'Sabine Lebrun marries — a man!', on the other hand, begins in the first person plural, which once more tries to inveigle the support of the reader by starting the article with three engaging rhetorical questions — more of which later. The article then reports the latest antics of the celebrity, so uses third person, apart from the aside about her boyfriend inexplicably liking Lady GaGa.

There are two main semantic fields in 'Pink Punk Princess?': there are a lot of words to do with nationality ('Canadian', 'British' and 'French-speaking Canada'), which are typical of the racist rants of this particular newspaper, and there are also a lot of words on the subject of how 'pink' Lebrun is. There are four mentions of this word and it relates to one of the paper's hobby-horses: sexuality and teenagers. The use of these semantic fields successfully allows the reporter to hone in on two main rallying calls for this paper, which will resonate with its faithful readership who will agree with the views entirely.

MUSIC

Pink Punk Princess?

Both articles are relatively informal in their use of language. 'Pink Punk Princess?' is the slightly more informal of the two, with the first paragraph setting the tone through its play on words with Lebrun's first name. This is carried on into the final paragraph, where the informal playing with Lebrun's first name continues, which engages the reader's interest.

'Sabine Lebrun marries — a man!' is equally informal with its use of the first person plural in the first paragraph, but it is the direct address to the readership that appears to be most inappropriately informal. There is one bracketed aside about her boyfriend, and the postscript at the end stresses the point that this newspaper thinks the whole affair was just a publicity stunt — some allegation by a newspaper that relies upon the misdemeanours of the famous to sell copies.

Finally, both articles rely upon various linguistic and rhetorical devices to achieve their effects. 'Pink Punk Princess?' uses several devices in a very heavy-handed way, for example the use of alliteration in the first paragraph with the word 'pink', which continues in the next-to-last paragraph. The repetition of the 'p' sound almost makes the writer appear to be beside himself with anger as he tuts at Lebrun's behaviour. 'Sabine Lebrun marries — a man!' tends to use rhetorical devices, such as the rule of three and rhetorical questions, to some effect. The very obvious rule of three in the first paragraph would put Obama to shame. It helps to reiterate how often the reader has seen reports of Lebrun's behaviour over the past few weeks. The final sentence is a rhetorical question which has the effect of making it obvious to the reader what the journalist thinks is the real reason behind Lebrun's antics over the past weeks.

Examiner's comment

There are other aspects of language in both articles that the student could have written about, but he/she has sensibly limited his/her response because of time constraints. This is a perfectly weighted response. Let's see how it fulfils the A* skills required.

Full and detailed understanding

The student has written the fullest possible answer in the time available. It is notable that A* students certainly give the impression of having more time than other students. You could compare an A* performer to a star footballer, who always seems to have more time to make a pass than his team-mates. A* students achieve this by imposing a structure on their response. The table you prepared in Task H would certainly have helped with this.

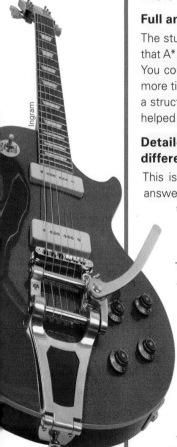

Detailed interpretation and analysis of how the writers use language differently to achieve their effects

This is undoubtedly a detailed response, but detail alone would only just place an answer into the top band of marks. To secure an A*, the student has focused on 'how the writers use language to achieve effects'. The highlighted sentences show examples of this.

Relevant quotation/reference

This student carefully roots all of his/her points in the text through either quotation or reference.

Focus on comparison and cross-referencing between the texts throughout the response

The student's comparisons are made throughout the text as a result of the structure of the answer. Rather than simply using discourse markers, the student has chosen the more sophisticated approach of cross-referencing each point with the other. This answer would receive full marks. It is exemplary and a pleasure to read.

Remember: if you are referring to a device, you don't need to quote it in its entirety. A simple reference will do the job.

AO2(ii) and AO2(iv)

Develop and sustain interpretations of writers' ideals and perspectives

Understand texts in their social, cultural and historical contexts

Key words	What the key words mean for A* students
develop and sustain	go into detail about specific points
interpretations	different meanings or understandings with the necessary use of relevant quotation to back up any such explanations
perspectives	points of view, or ways of seeing things
social, cultural and historical perspectives	how the texts fit into the period they were written in and whether they agree with or contradict any ways of seeing things at that time

Developing and sustaining your response

To develop and sustain a response you don't necessarily have to write a lot. Instead, you should write in detail about a number of aspects of the text, in relation to the text. That number may be as few as three. It is perfectly possible to show all of the required A* skills after having developed and sustained a response about a limited number of points.

You are not expected to 'develop and sustain' your response when under examination conditions in Unit 1. This is a skill that can only be assessed under controlled assessment, which is a halfway house between traditional examination and coursework. Don't worry that this new form of assessment is not as polished as coursework used to be, but it is even more important that you plan your response to address the A* skills required.

Social, cultural and historical perspectives

You do not have to be a historian or sociologist to answer the perspectives aspect of AO(iv). You should think about perspectives (such as the role of women in the text you have studied) and give your personal view. Merely adding a conclusion that addresses these issues will not suffice for an A/A*.

Controlled assessment

For the controlled assessment for Unit 3 part a: understanding written texts, A* students should play an integral part in the contextualisation of the task sent out by the board in January and June each year. This means that you should have a say in the actual wording of the task you are doing. Yes, that's right: you should be party to the writing of your own questions! You have to study a whole text from any genre, including non-fiction. A poetry text must consist of about 15 poems (a cluster from the Anthology, for example)

Ingram

and a prose text must be the equivalent of a novel or seven short stories. The text could be the same as one you are studying for the English Literature examination.

You don't have to write about all parts of the text. The guidance word limit is 1,200 words, or about 4 sides of handwriting, which has to be produced under formal supervision in a time totalling up to 4 hours.

You will have a choice of two tasks: **themes and ideas** or **characterisation and voice**.

Task I

Explore the ways the central characters are presented and developed in the text you have studied.

Example: How does Shakespeare use language to explore the relationship between Lady Macbeth and Macbeth? The key scenes you should refer to are 1v, 1vii, 2ii, 3ii, 5i and 5v.

Remember: contextualisation means putting this task within the context of the text you have studied.

Task J

Read through the students' plan below in response to Task I and identify where the student intends to make a 'detailed and perceptive analysis' of how language is used.

Remember: you are allowed to take brief notes into the formal assessment period, but they cannot include detailed planning grids or a pre-prepared draft. Make sure that your notes are checked before you begin to use them.

Student response to Task I

Plan
Focus on four small sections in only four scenes: 1v 36–52, 2ii 8–24, 5i 30–54 and 5v 16–2.

- 1v 36–52: soliloquy where LM is in control of language, e.g. images, poetic devices (e.g. alliteration, rhythm, etc.) Similar in rhythm and cadence to witches' chants. Concentrated and 'together'.

- 2ii 8–24: the opposite to the previous scene. Disjointed and suggests lack of control and panic. LM still the dominant partner — this position is continued throughout Act 3, e.g. the banqueting scenes.

- 5i 30–54: LM has lost control — this is shown by reversion to prose and lots of short sentences and questions, like M in 2ii.

- 5v 16–27: a relatively short speech, but very controlled: too controlled? M now has control of language and is relishing the thought of a fight — that's what he's good at and it has focused his mind.

Topfoto

Lady Macbeth seizes the dagger from Macbeth just after he has killed Duncan in Act 2, Scene ii

Extract from student response, showing insight

In her speech in 1v, Lady Macbeth fully engages the audience with her unnatural imagery, like 'Come to my woman's breasts/And take my milk for gall.' However, the rhythm of this speech is very similar to the rhythm of the witches' chants earlier in the Act.

Examiner's comment

To reach Grade C and above, you must show insight when discussing the features of a text. Insight means moving beyond the obvious.

This response certainly does more than simply re-tell the story. However, to achieve an A*, it is not enough to simply write a list of insightful thoughts. You have to show higher-grade skills, which in this case means to **analyse**.

Extract from student response, showing analysis

Shakespeare may have done this for several reasons, for example to subliminally link Lady Macbeth with the witches in the audience's mind. This would have been particularly relevant in the social, cultural and historical context of the play. Any woman who voices such views about her own breasts, which are meant to nourish and nurture, must be deranged or a witch. Shakespeare makes this link via the language; it may not have the same number of beats in a line, but it certainly has the same rhythm. Straightaway, Shakespeare's contemporary audience will have formed a view of Lady Macbeth due to these connotations.

The strict iambic pentameter of the former scene is broken in 2ii, where Shakespeare uses the broken language of lines 8–24 to show the utter panic of Macbeth, contrasted with the relative calm of Lady Macbeth.

Examiner's comment

To reach Grade B and above, your responses must include analysis. Analysis means examining more interpretations; looking at the effects of language in this case, structures and so on; considering the success of elements like dramatic devices; examining layers of meaning; and interpreting the play within a social and historical context.

Remember: you only have up to 4 hours for this assessment, so you must be realistic about what you can achieve. You need to further contextualise a task so that you can access the higher bands of marks. In personalising a task by contextualising it to only certain parts of the text, you will be more likely to be able to focus on the question and the necessary skills.

This response moves into analysis and begins to 'develop and sustain' a response by looking at how language is used by Shakespeare. By focusing on only four relatively small sections, this student has been able to develop a perceptive comment about rhythm, and the ways that Shakespeare shows the change in relationship through the change in the structure of the language.

Additionally, the student has incorporated comments about the social, historical and cultural background into the response, rather than tacking them onto the end.

> **Task L**
>
> Finish off the student's answer to Task I as a practice for your own controlled assessment.

Assessment for learning

In groups, read through each other's responses and identify where, and if, there is evidence of higher-level skills.

Here is a mark scheme for Grades A/A*:

- offers full and detailed understanding and interpretation of the play
- shows a detailed and perceptive appreciation, interpretation and analysis of how Shakespeare has used language to show the changing relationship
- offers full and relevant quotation in support of ideas with appropriate and perceptive comments
- focuses on social, cultural and historical perspectives in an integrated way

Macbeth and the three witches

Reading

Chapter 2

Writing an examination paper

A* students should be valued and used as 'experts' within a school. As only around 5% of students gain an A*, each school usually has a relatively small group of up to 10 A* students.

As a potential A* student, your English Department may want you to:

- act as an expert in speaking and listening scenarios, giving support and guidance to other students
- help students to contextualise the controlled assessments in English, English Language and English Literature
- write examination papers for your own school, or area

The final suggestion has many benefits:

use of localised issues as the stimulus material for texts used for Unit 1 in English/English Language

greater understanding of the central nature of the AOs in the production of exam papers

greater understanding of the way that questions focus on particular AOs

greater understanding of the links between AOs and the descriptors used in mark schemes

Writing your own questions

Here's a reminder of the four different question types:

(1) retrieval (4 marks)

(2) presentation (8 marks)

(3) inference (8 marks)

(4) comparison/language (16 marks)

You should try to find your own passages for students to write questions about, or write your own. This could be practice for English Language Unit 3 part (b): producing creative texts.

In the exam, you will be given three passages to work from. Use the passage below as practice. It is written in the style of Bill Bryson's book *Notes From A Small Island*.

Wigan pie-eaters

Getty

I suppose that the reason I went to Wigan was to make up my own mind about a place that has always been looked upon as a joke. Anyway, I'll let you decide.

First, let's show the bad sides of the place. I arrived in Wigan by train. They were obviously holding some sort of audition for circus sideshows. People had come from far and wide to try for the stall exhibiting the 'most bizarre eating habits'. I had already seen three sure finalists before I reached the first crossing.

I am not the best of eaters on the hoof, but some of these shell-suited warriors needed a bit of practice by the evidence of the gravy dribbling down their chins. Yes, chins: they had more than one. George Orwell reported that Wigan's youth were small and weedy when he visited in the 1930s, but they'd made up for it in the meantime: they were enormous! What would George have made of them?

Now let's look at the good sides. Wigan used to be known for coal, but now its fame rests on the shoulders of its richest inhabitant: JJB Sports. There were stores all over town; there was a huge warehouse built on former mine workings; an enormous stadium for the JJB sponsored and owned football team dwarfed the nearby retail outlets; a massive gym and Soccer Dome complex stood on the edge of some wasteland — and t'owner lived up t'road. Actually, he did and he'd brought a lot of jobs to Wigan, so I didn't hold that it was a long and winding road against him.

Sport is hugely important to this proud town, so it was no surprise to see that most of the youngsters were wearing football or rugby shirts. However, they didn't go as far as wearing body armour and shoulder pads in the streets. Most of the boys wore sports shirts as well, but they appeared to make you walk in a particular way: the 'Wigan Walk'. This used to refer to leaving a rugby match 5 minutes before the end when you were sure your side had won. This modern 'Wigan Walk' was more of a rolling swagger that announced that you were quite happy with yourself, thank you. It also allowed you to eat your pies at a leisurely pace without dribbling.

I couldn't visit Wigan without taking a trip to the local heritage sites, so I jumped on a bus to Hindley to visit the Monaco Ballroom. This was the centre of the Wigan section of the Northern Soul Scene in the 1960s and 1970s. However, nowadays Hindley is full of worn-out-looking old men in flat caps and beige zippered Marks & Spencer's jackets. The women had unlikely-coloured hairdos and the loose, phlegmy laughs of hardened smokers who now used the Monaco Ballroom for bingo. I liked them, though, because what you saw was what you got, and they were unfailingly friendly and content with their lot. They all called each other 'darlin' or 'love', with not a 'babe' to be heard.

That reminded me: my train was at 16.35 and I had to be getting back to Wigan Wallgate Station for the next stage of my journey in search of England's dark satanic mills. Surely there'd be some in Bolton. As I left, I was told to button my coat up, because it would be a 'top-coat colder' in Bolton. What was my final conclusion about Wigan? I liked the place because I liked the people and I liked the way it had developed. My kind of town, Wigan.

Task A

Think of two questions you could ask about the passage. One should be a retrieval-type question (4 marks) and the other an inference-type question (8 marks). Refer back to the questions earlier in this book as examples to follow.

Task B

Either: Go online and find a passage that lends itself to questions about presentation (8 marks) and comparison/language (16 marks). Write one of each kind of question.

Or: Produce your own webpage or promotional flier which gives a more up-beat and positive view of Wigan.

Reading

Chapter 3

English Literature: drama and prose

Reading in English Literature is assessed by almost exactly the same Assessment Objectives as for English/English Language.

Chapter 1 looked at the controlled assessment for English Language Unit 3 part (a): understanding written texts. The text the example referred to was *Macbeth* (see pp. 17–18). The text you are studying for the controlled assessment for English Literature Unit 3: the significance of Shakespeare and the English Literary heritage will link with this.

You ought to be studying the same text for both the reading controlled assessment in English Language and the reading controlled assessment in English Literature. The tasks chosen may be different, but the example in Task A uses the question from Chapter 1.

Task A

Explore the ways the central characters are presented and developed in the texts you have studied.

Example: How does Shakespeare use language to explore the relationship between Lady Macbeth and Macbeth? The key scenes you should refer to are 1v, 1vii, 2ii, 3ii, 5i and 5v.

And:

How does Dickens use language to explore the relationship between Pip and Magwitch, the convict in Great Expectations?

Remember: contextualisation means putting this task within the context of the texts you have studied.

Topfoto

Pip and Magwitch in a Royal Shakespeare Company production in 2005

We have already looked at the first part of this question, relating to *Macbeth*, from an English Language point of view, so we will now look at the second half as it relates to English Literature. Notice how this task's contextualisation almost forces you to address AO2: 'Explain how language, structure and form contribute to writers' presentation of ideas, themes and settings.' This AO has a high weighting (25–35% of the total marks), so it is vital that you demonstrate it to achieve an A*.

Student response to Task A

Plan

Focus on two small sections.

Chapter 1: the opening pages:
- Dickens creates atmosphere (almost like a horror story?) through language choices and we are naturally on Pip's side, as he is a needy orphan frightened by the convict
- long sentences lull the reader into a false sense of monotony
- 'Hold your noise!' is a linguistic shock after the 120-ish-word-long sentence that precedes it with no speech

Task B

Read through the student's plan in response to Task A and identify where the student intends to make a 'detailed and perceptive analysis' of how language is used in both *Macbeth* and *Great Expectations*.

- repetition of 'a man' and the connective 'and' to emphasise the convict's bizarre and terrifying appearance

Chapter 39: the opening pages:

- utilise pathetic fallacy, similar to the pathetic fallacy of the opening chapter, but for the opposite reasons — this language is meant to show a change in the relationship

- lots of action words at the outset in contrast with the monotony of Chapter 1

- conversation is more studied and the convict is in control and more 'civilised', even though Pip is repelled by him

- convict still speaks ungrammatically: 'It's disapinting...arter having looked for'ard'

> **Remember:** you do not have to make a detailed comparison in this task. Instead, you should draw a link between the two texts, which can be as little as a mention in the introduction and the conclusion. The contextualised task and the choice of texts makes the link implicit, and that is enough.

Extract from student response

Just as Shakespeare uses language to show the change in relationship between Macbeth and Lady Macbeth, so Dickens uses language to show an equally fluid and changing relationship between Pip and the convict. The language of prose is not as demonstratively poetic as that of Shakespeare's dramatic language, but there are enough linguistic devices to point the reader in the direction that Dickens wishes.

AlienCat/Fotolia

For example, the whole of the first page of the novel is written in relatively monotonous long sentences, which describe the monochrome vista of the fenlands that confronts Pip in the graveyard. After a particularly long sentence (approximately 120 words), the reader is shocked linguistically by a three-word exclamation in direct speech: 'Hold your noise!'

As if this wasn't enough of a linguistic shock, Dickens then heaps on the devices by using repetition and the rule of three to describe the convict in all of his battered glory. The repetition of active verbs — 'soaked', 'smothered', 'lamed', 'cut', 'stung' and 'torn' — thrusts this larger-than-life character into the reader's psyche after the purposeful lull of the opening page. This man is not dead and buried like Pip's immediate family, but as active as an active verb. The repetition of 'a man' three times also cranks up the rhetorical/linguistic devices. This is no wimp who 'gave up trying to get a living, exceedingly early in that universal struggle', but 'a man', unlike the bullied Joe Gargery, who is going to get his own way.

Dickens also uses language to place this convict socially. At the time, convicts were sent to Australia as a punishment and Magwitch has escaped from the convict ship, hence his appearance 'in coarse grey' and 'with a great iron on his leg'. Dickens lets us know later in the novel that the convict was tricked by Compeyson (who also cheated on Miss Havisham) and was part of the suffering sub-class for whom Dickens felt so much compassion. This compassion was as a result of his life experiences with his own father, which he recycles in several of his novels, e.g. *Little Doritt*.

Dickens cleverly uses the convict's language to place him in a lower social class than Pip, who speaks perfectly grammatically, even though his sister is only married to a blacksmith. The whole point of the novel is that Pip always thought he was better than this and hence he accepted his 'Great Expectations' with open arms, only to be so disappointed in Chapter 39. By putting such words as 'you little devil' and 'pint' into the convict's mouth, Dickens gives the reader the relative social condition of the two characters. This position is reiterated linguistically in Chapter 39 with words like 'disapinting' and 'arter', as the convict voices his 'disapintment' that Pip has not realised from whom his 'Great Expectations' have emanated: not Miss Havisham, as Pip had hoped, but from Estella's father — Magwitch, the convict on the run from his bondage in Australia.

It is to Chapter 29 that I will now shift the focus. As in the first chapter, the atmospheric conditions have a bearing on the action, but this time there is a storm that is a precursor for the storm about to descend on Pip's life. As in the first chapter, Pip is haunted by 'the footstep of my [his] dead sister', but this time there is a real ghost who is coming to haunt him — Magwitch.

As mentioned earlier, Dickens uses language to link this apparition with the convict whose name Pip never learned. There is not only the social difference between Pip's educated language and the way that Magwitch refers to Pip as

'Master', but the way Magwitch masterfully drip-feeds nuggets of information about Pip's income and circumstances that shift the power to the convict when he finally exclaims: 'Yes, Pip, dear boy. I've made a gentleman on you! It's me wot has done it!'

This is not the language of Miss Havisham, Estella or Jaggers. This is the language of Joe. After all his efforts to escape the linguistically starved background of the blacksmith's forge, Pip has been bankrolled by a convict. It is now almost too late for Pip to be forgiven, and though he does make amends, he is finally rebuffed linguistically when he goes back home to marry Biddy, the one person who was his linguistic equal at the forge — only to find out that she is not working at the school where she is mistress on the day he arrives: "'It's my wedding day,' cried Biddy, in a burst of happiness, 'and I am married to Joe!'" This is the final letdown for Pip, as Biddy has now married the virtual village idiot. Only now does Pip learn that you cannot judge people by outward appearances, such as use of language: you value them for their qualities. And he is happier for it in his more equable friendship with Estella in the revised ending.

In conclusion, both Shakespeare and Dickens use language to map characters' progressions throughout their works. Macbeth, after his confident beginning with the witches, is no match linguistically for his wife, but the control of the language shifts until Macbeth is bullishly praising his wife and bemoaning her death before his final battle in 5v. Dickens also uses language to map Pip's embarrassment at Joe's linguistic poverty, from the time when it was their 'evening habit to compare the way we bit through our slices [of bread], by silently holding them up to each other's admiration now and then', to the end of the novel, where Joe's last words are: 'O dear old Pip, old chap...God knows as I forgive you, if I have anythink to forgive!' Joe's language has not changed; Macduff's language has not changed: both Macbeth and Pip have changed and that change is mapped linguistically by both writers.

Examiner's comments

Remember that this is the second half of a piece of controlled assessment; the first half is discussed on pp. 17–18.

Controlled assessment is not coursework, nor is it externally assessed examination work: it is a halfway house between the two. This piece of work reflects the peculiar position between these modes of assessment: it has not got the polished perfection of over-worked coursework, nor has it got the necessarily narrow focus of an examination response. However, if we look at the Assessment Objectives, this response satisfies them in enough detail to reach the top band of marks. Examples of where the AOs are demonstrated have been highlighted throughout the response.

Here is a reminder of the AOs:

- **AO1:** Respond to texts critically and imaginatively; select and evaluate relevant textual detail to illustrate and support interpretations.
- **AO2:** Explain how language, structure and form contribute to writers' presentation of ideas, themes and settings.
- **AO3:** Make comparisons and explain links between texts, evaluating writers' different ways of expressing meaning and achieving effects.
- **AO4:** Relate texts to their social, cultural and historical contexts; explain how texts have been influential and significant to self and other readers in different contexts and at different times.

As mentioned earlier, AO2 is particularly important if you wish to gain a high grade. This student satisfies AO2 by keeping the question clearly in focus and showing full and detailed understanding and interpretation of the novel throughout. Nowhere does the response descend into mere paraphrase or storytelling, but 'relevant textual detail to illustrate and support interpretations'.

Here is a recap of the mark scheme for A/A*:

- offers full and detailed understanding and interpretation of the play/novel — this is obvious throughout the answer
- shows a detailed and perceptive appreciation, interpretation and analysis of how Shakespeare and Dickens have used language to show the changing relationships between Macbeth and Lady Macbeth and Pip and Magwitch
- offers full and relevant quotation in support of ideas with appropriate and perceptive comments
- focuses on social, cultural and historical perspectives in an integrated way

There is hardly a moment in this response where the student is not clearly on task and focusing on how language is used by the two writers.

The word limit for this answer is 1,200 words, so brevity and focus are key factors in achieving success. Another is the ability to come up with perceptive comments, and this student does so by writing a tightly argued appreciation of how language is linked with Dickens's overall aim.

The response would gain an A*.

Vladimir Melnikov/Fotolia

Reading

Chapter 4

English Literature: poetry

There are two routes through the English Literature specification: Route A and Route B:

- Route A requires you to complete Units 2 and 3. Poetry is assessed externally in Unit 2.
- Route B requires you to complete Units 4 and 5. Poetry is assessed via a controlled assessment in Unit 5.

You should have a say as to which route you take. Whether you choose Route A, which involves a 1 hour 15 minute exam, or Route B, which involves 4 hours of controlled assessment, will depend on your individual strengths and weaknesses.

Route A

Unit 2: poetry across time

This unit includes two sections:

- Section A: answer one question from a choice of two on the poetry cluster you have studied, in 45 minutes.
- Section B: answer a two-part question on one compulsory unseen poem in 30 minutes.

It is useful to prepare for Route A by:

- looking at one of the poems from the Anthology as an unseen and analysing its general principles
- comparing two of the poems from the Anthology which have many similarities in form, since they are both sonnets

Task A

Read 'Nettles' by Vernon Scannell. Then prepare some notes that you could use in a presentation as an 'expert' to another group in your class or school. These notes should give clear guidance as to how to approach an unseen poem, using the following sub-headings:

(1) What is your first impression of the poem's shape?

(2) Is there any sort of semantic field?

(3) Is there a rhyme scheme and how does it work?

(4) Are there any noticeable devices, like metaphors, alliteration etc. and how do they work?

(5) Is there some sort of change in the last line(s)? If so, what?

Nettles

My son aged three fell in the nettle bed.
'Bed' seemed a curious name for those green spears,
That regiment of spite behind the shed:
It was no place for rest. With sobs and tears
The boy came seeking comfort and I saw
White blisters beaded on his tender skin.
We soothed him till his pain was not so raw.
At last he offered us a watery grin,
And then I took my billhook, honed the blade
And went outside and slashed in fury with it
Till not a nettle in that fierce parade
Stood upright any more. And then I lit
A funeral pyre to burn the fallen dead,
But in two weeks the busy sun and rain
Had called up tall recruits behind the shed:
My son would often feel sharp wounds again.

Vernon Scannell

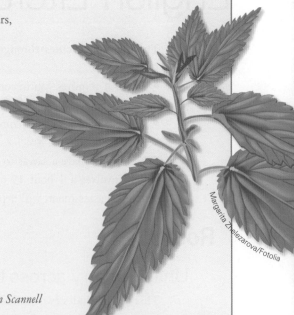

Margarita Zhelezarova/Fotolia

Remember: ask your teacher to show you what facilities there are in the Digital Anthology (such as Clozer and highlighting) for making your presentation more engaging.

Task B

Read the two sonnets below. Then compare their language, structure and form. You should concentrate on the words used, shape and the use of rhyme.

Sonnet 116

Let not to the marriage of true minds
Admit impediments. Love is not love
Which alters when it alteration finds,
Or bends with the remover to remove:
Oh no! It is an ever-fixed mark
That looks on tempests and is never shaken;
It is the star to every wandering bark,
Whose worth's unknown, although his height be taken.
Love's not Time's fool, though rosy lips and cheeks
Within his bending sickle's compass come:
Love alters not with his brief hours and weeks'
But bears it out even to the edge of doom.
If this be error and upon me proved,
I never writ, nor no man ever loved.

William Shakespeare

Sonnet 43

How do I love thee? Let me count the ways.
I love thee to the depth and breadth and height
My soul can reach, when feeling out of sight
For the ends of Being and Ideal Grace.
I love thee to the level of everyday's
Most quiet need, by sun and candlelight.
I love thee freely, as men strive for Right;
I love thee purely, as they turn from Praise.
I love thee with the passion, put to use
In my old griefs, ... and with my childhood's faith.
I love thee with the love I seemed to lose
With my lost Saints, – I love thee with the breath,
Smiles, tears, of all my life! – and, if God choose,
I shall but love thee better after death.

Elizabeth Barrett Browning

Task C

In a group, read through the notes in the table. Then:
- copy the table
- add new thoughts and ideas about shape and rhyme
- delete or change some of the thoughts and ideas

	'Sonnet 116'	'Sonnet 43'
Language	Connotations of marriage service in first two lines: recognisable to ordinary reader? Most of the words are simple, monosyllabic and easy to follow: nothing metaphysical or clever.	Bright, engaging opening with question and answer. Repetition used a lot which makes it almost prayer-like. Lots of religious connotations.
Structure	Chief pause in sense after line 12, but the rest of the poem is almost unstoppable, with emphasis on the final couplet. ababcdcdefefgg	Very different structure, with a novel rhyme scheme that keeps the poem tight and focussed. The structure is as close as a relationship. abbaabbacdcdcd
Form	The form is so predictable, formulaic and conventional that it is abnormal, and this is the key to the poem. The concept of love is easy for the poet to write about and this is stressed by the relatively simple form.	A little unconventional which reflects the later date and unconventional relationship?

Remember: A* students tend to disagree with what everybody else thinks, which is fine — so long as there is evidence in the texts to support your ideas.

Route B

Unit 5: exploring poetry

This unit has one task. You will be asked to make links between a range of poems from the English Literary Heritage text and Contemporary Poetry. The guidance word limit is 2,000 words under formal supervision, in time totalling up to 4 hours.

Task D

Either: Explore the ways the central characters are presented and developed in the texts/poems you have studied.

Or: Compare the ways that poets use language and form to present and develop central characters.

You can refer to the following poems from the 'Relationships' cluster in the Anthology — or to poems from one of the other clusters, if you prefer.

- 'Nettles' by Vernon Scannell
- 'Sister Maude' by Christina Rossetti
- 'Sonnet 116' by William Shakespeare
- 'Sonnet 43' by Elizabeth Barrett Browning
- 'To his Coy Mistress' by Andrew Marvell
- 'Singh Song' by Daljit Nagra (from the 'Character and Voice' cluster).

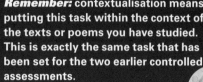

Remember: contextualisation means putting this task within the context of the texts or poems you have studied. This is exactly the same task that has been set for the two earlier controlled assessments.

Student response to Task D

Plan

Focus on small sections or aspects of each poem.

- 'Nettles': semantic field of soldiers and battle? Can't protect his son from life? War? Hurt in general? Rhyme scheme: ababcdcd, etc. Form is like a sonnet, but 16 lines: short, narrative?
- 'Sister Maude': same length and uses rhyme similarly, but is this autobiographical? Research. Short lines suggest a real hatred for this sister, which grows throughout the poem.
- 'Sonnet 116': very different in that it is an example of a 'marriage of true minds': compare similar rhyme scheme to 'Nettles' and very different relationship in 'Sister Maude'. Sonnet: ababcdcdefefgg
- 'Sonnet 43': similar to the strength of love in Shakespeare's 'Sonnet 116', but very different in its intensity of religious fervour. It also seems to be an unrequited love that can only be satisfied 'after death' for some reason.
- 'To his Coy Mistress': also deeply in love, but wants physical fulfilment. Rhyme scheme of aabb gives the poem inevitability (?), and we get to know more about the 'vegetable love' of the poet. Similar/different views about love to Shakespeare.
- 'Singh Song': delightfully different in most ways. Central character is the wife and the language mimics that of an Asian corner-shopkeeper. Engaging and vivid use of language. Similarities/differences with 'To his Coy Mistress'?

Task E

Copy out the sample plan from the student's response to Task D, then add to or take away from the notes. You could:

- concentrate on fewer poems, or different poems
- draw lines of similarity/difference in different colours

Remember to look for similarities and differences between language, structure and form. Discuss your choices with a group.

Task F

Use your extended notes from Task E to analyse similarities and differences in language, structure and form between your choice of poems.

Extract from student response

The central character of 'Sonnet 116' is the narrator, possibly Shakespeare, who is saying that his love 'looks on tempests and is never shaken'. This central character is trying to talk directly to the reader by using relatively simple language — the vast majority of the words in this poem are monosyllabic — and there are no difficult, or metaphysical, ideas. Shakespeare also wishes to engage the ordinary reader by his reference to the marriage service in the first two lines and by using homely images like the lighthouse in line 5, 'an ever-fixed mark' or 'star to every wandering bark'. These are images that the ordinary person would understand and appreciate, as are the references to the marriage service. It is almost as if Shakespeare wishes to sermonise the reader because the sonnet is in the third person: it is a generalised message that is clear and unequivocal.

This is very different from Marvell's 'To his Coy Mistress' and Browning's 'Sonnet 43'. Browning especially uses the sonnet form to suggest a thought process that is difficult and cleverly metaphysical, and which might put off the 'ordinary' reader. However, close study reveals a lot about the central character and her views about love. Rossetti, too, is totally enamoured of her love, but has been denied his love, in her opinion, by her sister. This is a vituperative poem that shows pure hatred for such a close relation:

'Who told my mother of my shame,
Who told my father of my dear?
Oh who but Maude, my sister Maude, Who lurked to spy and peer'

Such a long quotation has been used to exemplify the depth of feeling that the poet has for her sister. It is almost childish in its whingeing tone and use of simple language like 'spy and peer'.

Browning's poem looks similar on the page to Shakespeare's but is, in my opinion, more dense and difficult to follow than Shakespeare's, despite the fact that they have exactly the same form and a similar rhyme scheme. Why the difference? Well, I think that Browning is struggling to come to terms with a difficult relationship which cannot be consummated, 'I shall but love thee better after death'. This difficulty is manifested in the difficult, or metaphysical, nature of her thought processes. This is contrasted with the almost childlike repetition of 'I love thee'.

Natalia Hudyma/Fotolia

Examiner's comment

This response shows clear evidence of a detailed and perceptive appreciation, interpretation and analysis of how Shakespeare and Browning have used language to show changing or difficult relationships. To gain an A*, you have to show more insight and exploration. You can achieve this by avoiding any tendency to paraphrase or tell the story, and instead showing evidence of a convincing and imaginative interpretation.

Task G

Read 'Singh Song' by Daljit Nagra (available in the AQA Digital Anthology or in *Look We Have Coming to Dover!*, published by Faber & Faber). Then read the student response below to the question: 'How does this poem appeal to you?' and see how it 'takes off' as the student writes about a poem that appeals to him.

Student response to Task G

Since my grandparents came from the Indian sub-continent, I found Nagra's poem especially relevant to my own situation. However, here is a poet who is willfully writing in the persona of the son of a traditional Asian shop-keeper, who delights in shocking and affronting his parents via his bride, who is 'effing at my mum' and 'she have a red crew cut/and she wear a Tartan sari'. Is he proud of his wife? Well, the language would suggest that he is besotted with her as she *'Is priceless baby'* and he repeats the phrase, 'my bride', three times to accentuate this total love. This is despite the fact that she goes on Sikh lover sites pretending to offer herself for an arranged marriage.

However, it is in the language of this poem that the poet best conveys his feelings for the characters. The two main characters are one and they have 'sort of' adopted the Western lifestyle, but there is a gauche quality to the narrator's voice: 'Ve I return vid my pinnie untied'.

Is priceless baby

B

Speaking and listening

Assessment Objectives for speaking and listening

Under the topic of speaking and listening, you are required to show that you can speak clearly across a range of activities to different audiences. You will need to select appropriate vocabulary and be able to work with other people as well as on your own. Usually, your ability to communicate will be assessed orally, but your study of spoken language will be assessed in writing.

You will complete three different types of controlled assessments: presenting, discussing and listening, and role-playing. Each activity is marked separately. In total they are worth 20% of your final mark.

Speaking and listening is assessed against the following Assessment Objectives (AOs).

Pressmaster/Fotolia

English Language AO1: Speaking and listening	
AO1(i)	**Speak** to **communicate clearly** and **purposefully**; **structure** and **sustain** talk, adapting it to different situations and audiences; use standard English and a variety of techniques as appropriate.
AO1(ii)	**Listen** and **respond to speakers' ideas** and **perspectives**, and **how they construct** and **express meanings**.
AO1(iii)	**Interact** with others, **shaping meanings** through suggestions, comments and questions and **drawing ideas together**.
AO1(iv)	Create and sustain different roles.
English Language AO2: Study of spoken language	
AO2(i)	**Understand variations** in **spoken language**, **explaining** why **language changes** in relation to **contexts**.
AO2(ii)	**Evaluate the impact** of **spoken language** choices in their **own** and **others' use**.

AO1(i)

Speak to communicate clearly and purposefully; structure and sustain talk, adapting it to different situations and audiences; use standard English and a variety of techniques as appropriate

Key words	What the key words mean
communicate clearly and purposefully	You talk to an audience and explain how you think and feel about something.
structure and sustain	You organise your material into a logical order and speak at length about it.
adapting it	You change your language to fit the age and membership of your audience — a talk to a group of five-year-old children would have different language and presentation to one to your headteacher.
use standard English	You use the kind of language you would be expected to use in written tests.

Grade A/A*	A personal response which covers the topic in detail and includes sophisticated vocabulary while using standard English appropriately.

Remember: when you are speaking, you must decide what the audience needs to know, what evidence you can supply to back up your views, and how to make it interesting.

Ullswater Community College

English Dept

No:

Task A

Read the extract below, which comes from an interview for a headteacher's post. It is the candidate's response to the question, 'What is your vision for the school?'

Give a talk to the rest of your class explaining the changes you would make to your school if you were headteacher.

'Change? Who needs it? I have examined this school in detail and my considered opinion is that you do. Need change, I mean.

'Why? I believe that schools are for the students. It is the students who should be at the heart of all of our important decisions. Not only that, they should be involved in making those decisions. It would be my intention, if appointed as headteacher, to consult widely with students about what they consider to be the strengths and weaknesses of the school.

'Having been round the school this morning, it is clear that its fabric is in a deteriorating condition. The amount of litter is intolerable and the state of the toilets is a disgrace, bordering on a health hazard. I believe these should be priorities for financial investment. I expect the highest possible standards from our students. How can we expect them to perform highly and respect their environment if we do not give them the best?

Alan Reed/Fotolia

'The range of subjects we offer our students is too narrow. Lessons should encourage students to participate, to enjoy and to achieve. We need to design an experience that is exciting and relevant for all of our students. I envisage far-reaching reforms for the curriculum. Diplomas would be central to our planning. I want children to want to come to this school so I would offer them exciting events both in and outside school, refreshing approaches to teaching, and the opportunity to develop to their maximum potential.'

Student response to Task A

What's it like to play at being God? Some people think that's what headteachers do. They control the lives of hundreds of people. If they get it right everyone benefits. If they get it wrong…

I don't intend to get it wrong. A headteacher's job is all about making choices. To do that, they need information. My choices will be made using the best possible information — my experience. I know this school in detail. I know the places the bullies haunt like gruesome ghouls. I know how horrible school meals are. I know how uncomfortable the uniform is. I will do a fantastic job because, as my mother says, like every teenager, I know it all!

Doubtless you think you could do just as well. Let's face it: we are all experts on education. We have been immersed in it since our early years. That means you'll be able to appreciate the complexity of the job I'm going to do. Lessons, buildings, uniform… They all need attention. In fact, some of them need a magic wand.

So what's my motivation for all this? It isn't to play God. It's to make life better for everyone, and if I do that I'll benefit as much as anyone else. Unfortunately I'm not Harry Potter. I need you to work with me. Just consider our potential. Some people try to *use* magic. Together we can *be* magic.

Examiner's comment

The speaker's main ideas are cogently expressed, using standard English and a varied vocabulary. There are clear attempts to connect with the audience through the opening question and use of the word 'you'. The rhetorical questions force the audience members to consider their own opinions. Irony is used effectively.

Although the speaker makes a series of points, none of them are expanded fully. The thinking behind the ideas is explained clearly, but the candidate has not actually identified the changes to be made. Nevertheless, this answer would fulfil most of the Grade A descriptors.

How to improve

To achieve a Grade A*, the candidate needs to develop some of the points more and attempt to create a more inventive organisation of the material.

Assessment for learning

Read the third paragraph again. Identify opportunities for the student to expand upon the points being made. Discuss your findings with a partner and rewrite the paragraph.

Task B

Write a response to Task A that will get you at least a Grade A.

Remember: there are three parts to this activity: the opening, your ideas and explanations, and the ending. They are all important.

Assessment for learning

Exchange your response to Task B with another student and assess whether you think theirs explains what they think and why. Decide whether it would keep the audience's interest. Now write notes to explain to your partner how they can improve what they have written.

Student response to Task B

Opening

Can you feel something itching? I can. It's making me want to scratch. Perhaps you feel the same. I want to scratch away at the surface of this school to reveal to you the depth of the disease I have discovered here. As I sit inside this antiquated building, I feel I like I am presiding over a geriatric patient whose terminal illness has not been revealed to them. In my opinion, this school should have been retired on grounds of ill-health. So what should we do? Should we humour the tumour? You may not like what I have to say but I have a Doctorate of Philosophy in Educational Management, so I am well equipped to diagnose a remedy.

Ending

So do I have a panacea or a placebo? I have made my prognosis. The choice is between a short-term fix and a long-term cure. Not everything will be palatable. The best medicine often tastes obnoxious. To cut out a cancer, you have to use a very sharp scalpel. Take my hand and come with me into my Theatre of Dreams. Trust me. I'm a doctor.

Dušan Zidar/Fotolia

Examiner's comment

This candidate uses a range of techniques to draw the audience into the speech and to maintain interest. There is confident use of the word 'you' in both the opening and ending. This makes the listener feel part of the talk. There is clever use of a variety of sentence lengths, for instance at the start of the opening. This is an individual response and the character of the speaker comes across clearly. This is original and takes the risk of alienating its audience by pointing out uncomfortable realities from the outset. It is calculated and balanced, using a range of devices, including alliteration, metaphor, irony and comparison. Its tone at the end is comforting, offering the security of the speaker's experience. The speech is sophisticated in its use of grammar, vocabulary and the way it communicates complex ideas. The use of the medicine metaphor is sustained throughout the talk and is used as the main vehicle to highlight the speaker's priorities, views and perspectives. Possibly the only thing lacking is evidence of a clear attempt to use humour.

This candidate's work is worthy of a Grade A*.

AO1(ii)

Listen and respond to speakers' ideas, perspectives and how they construct and express their meanings

Remember: when you are speaking, you must explain fully, but give other people the chance to speak too. When you are listening, show your understanding through your body language and your spoken responses.

Key words	What the key words mean
respond to speakers' ideas	You listen to what other people say and make comments on it or question it.
perspectives	You understand what people are trying to say and ask questions to make sure.
how they construct and express meanings	You look for examples of bias or prejudice in what people say.

Grade A/A*

You manage your group/pair by listening carefully and asking questions to find out exactly what is meant while also putting forward your own thoughts and encouraging other people to take part in order to complete the task fully and on time.

Task C

In pairs, write the lyrics for a song for either Sabine Lebrun or Will Swift. You can find further information about Sabine Lebrun in Section A of this book. Will Swift records for the same record company. Use their CD covers and song lists to help you.

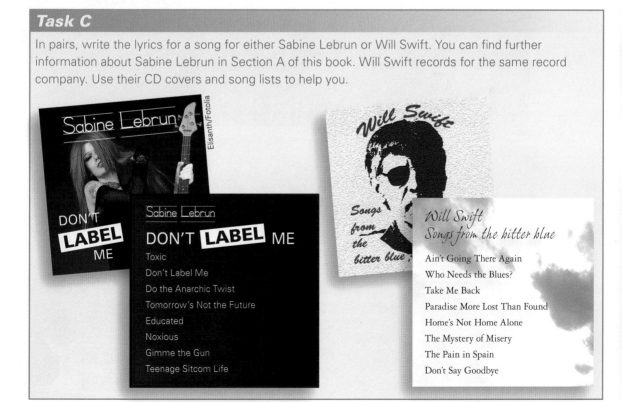

Sabine Lebrun
DON'T LABEL ME

Sabine Lebrun
DON'T LABEL ME

Toxic
Don't Label Me
Do the Anarchic Twist
Tomorrow's Not the Future
Educated
Noxious
Gimme the Gun
Teenage Sitcom Life

Will Swift
Songs from the bitter blue

Will Swift
Songs from the bitter blue

Ain't Going There Again
Who Needs the Blues?
Take Me Back
Paradise More Lost Than Found
Home's Not Home Alone
The Mystery of Misery
The Pain in Spain
Don't Say Goodbye

Elisanth/Fotolia

Task D

In pairs, discuss who you think the target audience would be for each CD.

'Gimme the Gun' refers to a sensitive topic that merits serious consideration and discussion. An additional activity might be for students to research and discuss the negative impacts of gun crime on society.

Task E

Read the lyrics for 'Gimme the Gun' by Sabine Lebrun and 'Don't Say Goodbye' by Will Swift. With your partner, compare the styles of the two performers. Together, write the lyrics for another song from one of the CDs.

Remember: there are two parts to this activity — speaking and listening. *What* you decide is not important. *How* you reach your decision is vital.

Gimme the Gun

My mom's a junkie and my dad's a drunk
They look down on me because I'm a punk!
So I just hang out with my good friend, Dan.
He ain't very much but at least he's my man.

So we cruise on out to the liquor store.
My head says 'No' but my body says 'More'.
So Dan goes in with his fake ID.
That's when he decides he prefers it for free.

Can't remember when I had such fun
Bang, Bang, Bang, Bang.
Gimme the gun!

So we get away like Bonnie and Clyde
It's like hide and seek but there's nowhere to hide.
The radio's playing an APB
The description's of Dan and of someone like me.
So we try to run but we don't get far.
This ain't no Ferrari, it's Dan's Dad's car.

Can't remember when I had such fun
Bang, Bang, Bang, Bang.
Gimme the gun!

There's a roadblock up ahead and a searchlight in my eyes.
It's a turkey shoot and we're first prize.
There's a sergeant with a bullhorn and he's preaching and praying
But my mind can't make out much of what he's saying.

Dan's got a grin on his face from ear to ear
A cross 'tween a smile and a bit of a sneer.
When he looks like that I know there's nothing to fear,
He'll get us out, he'll get us into the clear.

Can't remember when I had such fun
Bang, Bang, Bang, Bang.
Gimme the gun!

Dan'll look after me, he'll take care
But when I look in the seat, Dan's not there.
The cop's giving it loud and he's giving it large.
That's when I realise that I'm in charge.
If I want some more fun I just have to decide,
So I pick up the gun and I step outside.

Can't remember when I had such fun
Bang, Bang, Bang, Bang.
Gimme the gun!

Can't remember when I had such fun
Bang, Bang, Bang, Bang.

Don't Say Goodbye

You tell me that it's over and that
you haven't found another
But I can't seem to understand.
Why leave if there's no lover?
You've been my heart and soul since
I can't remember when
Can't we give it one last go and start it all again?

Please don't leave and make me cry
Turn around, don't say goodbye.
Don't leave if there's no other guy
Just turn around, don't say goodbye.

When everything is said and done there's
much more said than has been done
I can't believe that there's no one.
Why leave when there's no other?
If you go now you'll take away the sweetest romance
Can't we give it one more go, one last chance?

Please don't leave and make me cry
Turn around, don't say goodbye.
Don't leave if there's no other guy
Just turn around, don't say goodbye.

Yummy/Fotolia

Student response to Tasks D and E

Lisa: I think Sabine's audience is easy but Will Swift's is really difficult. It's hard to tell from the cover how old he is or what type of music he does.

Priya: Yes. Who do you think he is?

Lisa: Well, Sabine's Canadian and they both record for the same company, so I would guess he's Canadian or American as well. All of the song titles on his CD seem very depressing, so I don't think he's aiming at young people.

Priya: 'Gimme the Gun' is pretty depressing. That's aimed at young people. Mind you, so was the gun.

Lisa: True, but the song's not self-pitying. 'Don't Say Goodbye' is miserable and self-absorbed. Why would anyone want to stay with someone who says the only reason they shouldn't leave is because they haven't found someone else yet? How selfish is that? I see him as a middle-aged misery, singing songs for my dad. I like Sabine because she's young and she sings about things I can relate to. I think we should do one of her songs.

Priya: I agree. How are we going to decide which one?

Lisa: Let's look at the titles and see what springs to mind.

Priya: All right. What about 'Toxic'?

Lisa: OK. Any ideas?

Priya: Well, looking at the opening verse of 'Gimme the Gun', I think she likes to use irony, but I also think she likes to shock.

Lisa: A sort of rock shock?

Priya:	That's very good! I like that. That's given me an idea to link her with 'Toxic'.
Lisa:	What is it?
Priya:	Come on, work it out. What describes Sabine and rhymes with 'Toxic'?
Lisa:	Rock Chick!
Priya:	Exactly. How about, 'When you look at me you think I'm a rock chick, but mess with me and you'll find I'm toxic'?
Lisa:	That's brilliant.
Priya:	I thought so. Thank you, kind lady. Unfortunately, I can't think of any more.
Lisa:	How about we try to incorporate those ideas into one of the others? What about 'Don't Label Me'?
Priya:	Starting with?
Lisa:	The same kind of idea… 'You look at me and you think punk rock. Why should that be such a shock?' Can you think of anything else that we can identify with her?
Priya:	What about her clothes or what she looks like?
Lisa:	Good idea. Let's look at the pictures. What stands out?
Priya:	Her hair and her tights. They're both pink.
Lisa:	So what do you think of, 'I got my pink mesh tights, hair, matching highlights. I got a pin through my nose. Not got ribbons and bows'?
Priya:	That fits her personality perfectly. It's her completely.
Lisa:	That's given me the ending. 'When you look at me you get what see. So I won't label you if you don't label me!'

Examiner's comment

Although this is only the opening of the discussion, both candidates can be seen to be expressing their opinions and taking a full part. They work together and bounce ideas off each other. They praise and encourage each other. Each of them draws the other into the conversation by asking questions. These are also used to clarify meanings and get further information, to enable a full exploration of the topic.

Lisa expands fully on her ideas but Priya does not always do the same. The main ideas are clearly expressed in standard English, but Lisa is able to use non-standard English appropriately and effectively in imitating Lebrun's character in the lyrics. Both speakers explain their thinking, but Lisa contributes more to the completion of the task by responding inventively through imaginative explorations of the ideas.

If the discussion continued at this level, Priya would fulfil all of the Grade B descriptors and some of the Grade A ones, while Lisa would be moving towards a Grade A*.

How to improve

Lisa needs to create more opportunities for Priya to become further involved in the creative side of the discussion.

Assessment for learning

Start your discussion and talk to each other for 2 minutes. Then stop and tell your partners what they have done well and how they can improve. Start the discussion again and try to include all of the advice you have been given.

AO1(iii)

Interact with others, shaping meaning through suggestions, comments and questions and drawing ideas together

Key words	What the key words mean
interact	You take a full part in the activity and work with other people by listening to what they say and making comments on it or questioning it.
shaping meaning	You work through ideas together to develop them and express them in ways that you can all understand.
drawing ideas together	At the end of the task you go over all of the ideas to enable you come to a conclusion.

Grade A/A*	You manage your group/pair by listening carefully and asking questions to find out exactly what is meant while also putting forward your own thoughts and encouraging other people to take part in order to complete the task fully and on time.

Task F

In a pair or group, decide what a person living in 2050 would tell their grandchildren about life in the early twenty-first century.

Remember: there are two parts to this activity — speaking and listening. *What* you decide is not important. *How* you reach your decision is vital.

Student response to Task F

Kyle: Let's start by making a list of all the things we want to talk about. Then we can select which ones to use and sequence them.

Lucy: All right. You make your list and I'll make mine. Then we can compare.

They make their lists.

Kyle: What have you got?

Lucy: I've got lots of things, but I'm thinking we really should have our own opinions on them as well.

Kyle: You mean to explain and justify our inclusions?

Lucy: That's right. It should be a personal response, so I'd include something about my mum giving birth to my little brother.

Kyle: I'd include Hull City making history by getting into the Premier League for the first time in 2008, and losing the title of the biggest city in Europe never to have had a football team in the highest division.

Lucy: You'll probably have to explain what the Premier League was as well. You might even have to tell them what football was!

Kyle: What about including something big?

Lucy: Like 9/11?

Kyle: Yes, because that would give balance and contrast with the football, which seems trivial in comparison. I like that. So, let's make sure we've got it all sorted. What else do you think we should include?

Examiner's comment

This is only the beginning but both candidates take a full part and accept responsibility for moving the discussion on. Kyle directs questions at Lucy, enabling her to develop some of her ideas. He also uses these questions to clarify the meaning of what Lucy is saying. Kyle encourages Lucy to take control with the last statement which draws them back to the structure of their presentation. Lucy explains clearly what she thinks should be included but she does not really expand her ideas, almost presenting them as items in a list. Both students listen and respond engagingly to the other one, engaging with their ideas and feelings. To reach a Grade A, both students would need to initiate and sustain the discussion more. They would need to challenge each other's ideas instead of just accepting them. This would require more persuasion to take place.

Assessment for learning

When you are discussing, ask the other members of your group to grade your performance. Get them to tell you if you are doing enough.

> **Remember:** Make sure you contribute enough to score highly! When you are speaking, you must explain fully, but give other people a chance to speak too. When you are listening, show your understanding through your body language and your spoken responses.

AO1(iv)

Create and sustain roles

Key words	What the key words mean
create	You make up new characters or adapt existing ones.
sustain roles	You stay in character throughout an extended performance.

Grade A/A*	You create realistic, complex characters with more than one side to their personalities. You keep the audience's interest through the content and realism of your performance.

> **Remember:** when you are performing, you must stay in role as the character you are playing.

Task G

Read the extract from *Red Herrings* below. In a group, prepare an improvised performance for the rest of your class in which Inspector Groves questions the characters about their involvement in the death of Lord Ryedale. The Inspector should reveal the culprit and the clues at the end of the piece. The clues in the text should lead you to the killer, but if you can't work it out, it doesn't matter. Just make sure the Inspector has reasons for blaming whoever you decide is the murderer.

Remember: You need to make sure that everyone has a large enough role to score well.

Red Herrings

Ryedale Hall had always been an imposing building. In the dim half-light of an early September morning, the amber tentacles of sunlight caressed it like a long-lost lover, enveloping it with warmth and giving the old building an ethereal, gossamer appearance. Inspector Groves was well aware of the fairytale quality of the house. It was, he thought, in stark contrast to the grisly scene he would witness inside.

The Inspector rang the doorbell, then, turning his collar up again the chill wind, turned to view the splendour of the oval lawn, glowing golden in the gently growing light. A noise behind him brought the Inspector back to reality. He looked around as the oak-panelled doors swung wide to reveal the stocky figure of Ingrid Masters, the cook of the household. With very few formalities, the Inspector was ushered into the Great Hall, where four forlorn people awaited him. A glance around confirmed them as either members of the town's higher social order or as staff of Ryedale Hall. A scrutiny of their faces gave the Inspector the almost reassuring impression that a suicide made even these comfortable people uneasy.

Arranged around the room in an awkward gathering were Lady Melissa Ryedale, the deceased's widow; his heir and daughter, Julia Ryedale; Anton Charterhouse, his business partner; and Howard Adams, the butler. Ingrid Masters swept the Inspector past the mourners and up the stairs to the study, where nothing had been touched since the discovery of the body following the sound of two gunshots.

Lord Ryedale lay face down, his head towards the door. A crimson rivulet flowed from his stomach while bloody globules glistened round his mouth. The eyes, bulging with terror, reminded the Inspector faintly of a floundering fish. In the body's hand, a magnum revolver was tightly gripped. One chamber of the weapon was spent.

The study overlooked the rear of the house, the ornamental fish ponds, the rose garden and the tennis courts. The shadow cast by the house on this idyllic setting reflected the darkness of the case.

It seemed so straightforward, so obvious, and yet something gnawed at the Inspector's mind. Something was not right. Groves raised the unlocked sash-cord window to release the stench of death and clear his head. Looking down, he saw the peat filled rose-bed. The swiftness of the window closing again almost caught him by surprise. It slammed shut.

Returning to the Great Hall, a spinal icicle froze the Inspector's inners as what he had been trying to push aside finally asserted itself. A glacier of calm, his cold eyes pierced each of the people there, searching their inner beings. Of course, he thought, Lord Ryedale didn't kill himself. He was murdered! As he surveyed their faces, it occurred to him whimsically that all of them were trying to look innocent — but they all looked guilty. All he had to do was to piece together the clues to decide who killed Lord Harvey Ryedale.

Nikolai Sorokin/Fotolia

Witness statements

Lady Melissa Ryedale

I was agitated all night. I'd decided to tell Harvey that I wanted a divorce. I've been having an affair with Anton Charterhouse for some time and I'd finally decided to sort the whole thing out. I arranged to meet Anton in the Summer House after I'd explained everything to my husband.

It took a lot of courage to confront Harvey but I think he suspected anyway. I met him in the drawing room. His reaction was one of quiet astonishment. No screams, no hysterics. That wasn't his style. He steadfastly refused to discuss the matter. We decided to sleep in separate bedrooms and to talk again in the morning.

I felt relieved that the deception was over. I went to the bedroom to tidy myself up before I met Anton. That was the last time I saw Harvey alive. I didn't love him any more but I didn't kill him.

Anton Charterhouse

We'd all been invited to Ryedale for a meeting to discuss Harvey's forthcoming attempt to become a Member of Parliament at the next election. It went very smoothly and we were all extremely pleased by the outcome. We had been partners in an accounting business for a number of years and I was very pleased to be able to help him.

To be honest, I would have been delighted if Harvey had got himself trapped down in London. Melissa and I have been having an affair for some time and I felt he was getting suspicious. I'd decided it was time to bring it all out into the open.

I met Harvey in the Billiard Room. I presumed everyone else was in bed. We went up to his study on the pretext of having a drink. I told him how I felt and he accepted it. We were old friends, remember. He dropped into his swivel chair, somewhat deflated, as I left.

From there I went to the Summer House to await Melissa. Some time afterwards I heard two shots and ran quickly up the gravel path. My shoes were covered in mud but I didn't care. I thought Harvey had shot Melissa. I frantically rang the doorbell. The butler let me in.

I've lost a good friend tonight. I wanted Harvey out of the way but I didn't kill him.

Howard Adams

I've been the butler at Ryedale Hall for 6 years. During that time I like to think I've served his Lordship diligently. I've been suffering from a nervous disorder. I'm following a treatment of medication prescribed by my doctor. In the rush tonight I forgot to take my tablets with the result that I was very tense by the time the meal was ready. It's unusual for me to be careless but I slipped during the meal, covering her Ladyship in soup. His Lordship exploded and gave me a week's notice there and then.

After everyone had gone to bed, I started my rounds to make sure everything was locked up for the night. I realised his Lordship was in his study. I decided to go up and apologise, and ask for a second chance. On the way upstairs, I heard two shots, the first very loud, and the second, about 10 seconds later, quieter, as if fired from a distance. I ran upstairs and discovered the body.

I stood for some 30 seconds wondering what to do. Then the doorbell rang. I ran downstairs and met Mr Charterhouse. He was breathless and sweating.

I've always been loyal to my master and I didn't kill him.

Warren Millar/Fotolia

Julia Ryedale

Daddy and i didn't see eye-to-eye on a lot of things. We didn't get on very well at all. He was always so damned stuffy. i'd just got back from my final semester at UCLA in America and frankly i was bored to tears.

it appeared that Daddy had got wind of some of my antics state side and, predictably, was not amused. Some clown had put a video of me on YouTube. i met him in the library. He told me there were rumours about myself and a rather tasty American actor, isaac Mayhart. He asked me to deny them. when i said i couldn't, he told me i was no longer his heir and that he would cut me out of his will in the morning.

i was blazing mad and stormed out of the room. Later, when i had calmed down, i set off for his study to try to get him to change his mind. it was then that i heard a shot followed by something that sounded like someone being clubbed. i certainly didn't kill him.

Assessment for learning

As a group, decide which character is the killer and why. Each person needs to decide what they will say to the Inspector. Read your character's witness statement and the narrative, then make a list of the things you want to tell the Inspector. Discuss with your group what your reactions should be and what needs to be done to make them more realistic.

Writing a script is *not* allowed in the role-playing controlled assessment. This means you will have to improvise your performance — but you can still rehearse it. For each of the events in your improvisation, make a list of the things you are going to say and how you are going to say them. You should think about your movements and gestures.

Remember:
To make your performance realistic, you should show a range of emotions.

Student response to Task G

Adams: That's ludicrous! How could I be the killer? I was downstairs. Just because the butler always does it doesn't mean I did. Of course I didn't do it. Why would I?

Julia: Why wouldn't you? He'd sacked you. And not before time too. You've never been any good. If I'd been in charge, I'd have got rid of you ages ago. In fact, I would never have employed you. Did you ever find those references you couldn't produce when Daddy interviewed you?

Adams: That's a monstrous accusation! Well, you would say that, wouldn't you? You're just trying to impress the Inspector and divert the blame from yourself. Don't think I can't see through your little charade. All this 'Daddy' bit is just a thin veneer. I know what you thought of him and I know what you did in America with that uncouth youth.

John Takai/Fotolia

Julia: It was you who told him! What were you doing on YouTube?

Adams: Never mind that. You're just trying to set up another smokescreen. Have you told your mother about *your* affair with Mr Charterhouse?

Melissa: What?

Inspector: Can we stop just there? Now, Mr Adams, perhaps, without vitriol, you could take us through your version of the night's events.

Adams: I am not a criminal! To point the finger of suspicion at me is a weak attempt to deflect and divert attention away from the real murderer. My position in the household relies on trust. I refute these allegations unreservedly. Being butler makes me privy to many confidences and secrets. I am the eyes and the ears of the house. With that comes a weight of responsibility. Recently this has placed an intolerable strain on me…particularly with the indiscretions and infidelities of some members of the family. I have always performed my duties with dignity. Tonight…I made an unfortunate mistake for which the master…rightly…punished me. I was going to see him in his study to beg for clemency when I heard two gunshots; the first very loud and the second, about 10 seconds later, quieter, as if fired from a distance. I ran upstairs and discovered the body. Despite any appearances to the contrary, I am not the murderer. How could anyone suggest I am a killer? The only thing I have ever killed is time.

Examiner's comment

Most of the candidates are involved in this part of the improvisation, but they do not perform equally. Adams has a significant role, which is sustained and developed to move the drama on. The character interacts smoothly with the others, creating realistic confrontations. The complexity of the character is shown through the ways Adams reacts to the Inspector and the other characters, demonstrating different sides of his personality. There are plenty of opportunities for Adams to use a variety of verbal and non-verbal techniques. He uses sophisticated language while keeping the character convincing. Changes in tone and rhetoric emphasise the points he makes and his use of pauses shows how the character is grappling to find the right words to express his feelings. There are clear opportunities for movements and gestures.

The candidate goes beyond the descriptors for Grade A, as he/she uses a range of appropriate techniques to direct the response of the audience. Therefore, this candidate is worthy of a Grade A*. The other characters are less well developed and are limited to minor, supporting roles. The candidates would need to give a similar performance to Adams' in their own scenes if they are to achieve Grade A. For instance, it would be easy for the Inspector to receive a low grade; the candidate playing this role would need to take a leading role in drawing out information from the other characters.

Assessment for learning

When you are rehearsing, ask the other members of the group to grade your performance. Get them to tell you if you are doing enough and what they think you need to do to improve.

Speaking and listening

Chapter 6

Assessment Objectives for studying spoken language

The study of spoken language has completely changed. You will be asked to explain how language has developed; how it is used; its effects on other people; and how it is still changing. It is assessed according to AO2.

English Language AO2: Study of spoken language	
AO2(i)	**Understand variations** in **spoken language, explaining** why **language changes** in relation to **contexts**.
AO2(ii)	**Evaluate the impact** of **spoken language choices** in your **own** and others' **use**.

AO2(i)

Understand variations in spoken language, explaining why language changes in relation to contexts

Key words	What the key words mean
understand variations	You show that you know how spoken language is used for different outcomes.
explaining language changes	You can tell the examiner the reasons for the different uses of spoken English.
contexts	You understand how language changes to fit the age and membership of your audience, e.g. a discussion with your friends about how to plan a presentation to the rest of the class would have different language to the actual presentation itself.

Grade A/A*	A perceptive analysis of how you and other people use and adapt spoken English for different purposes using sophisticated interpretation, analysis and evaluations of your key data.

Where is AO2(i) assessed?

This AO is assessed in GCSE English Language Unit 3: understanding spoken and written language and writing creatively. It is specifically covered in Unit 3, part c: studying spoken language. This is worth 10% of your final marks.

How is AO2(i) assessed?

Your teacher will give you a controlled assessment. This could take place at any time during your course. Your work will be marked by your teacher and moderated by the examination board. This assessment can only be done in writing, and should be 800–1,000 words long.

Your teacher will set your task. It will cover three broad topic areas:
- social attitudes to text and language
- spoken genres
- multi-modal task

You will only do one assessment, so your response must cover both AO2(i) and AO2(ii).

AO2(ii)

Evaluate the impact of spoken language choices in your own and others' use.

Key words	What the key words mean
evaluate the impact	You analyse your evidence to show the effect of different types of spoken language.
spoken language choices	You can explain to the examiner what choices of language are being made and the reasons for the different uses of spoken English.
own and others' use	You understand how language changes to fit the age and membership of your audience — a discussion with your friends about how to plan a presentation to the rest of the class would have different language to the actual presentation itself.

Grade A/A*	A perceptive analysis of how you and other people use and regard accents using sophisticated interpretation, analysis and evaluations of your key data

Social attitudes to spoken language

Task A

Show how language use can influence our views of other people, and how spoken language can establish our identities and sometimes resist conformity.

First, you will need to canvas opinions on what your friends and family think about people who speak in different ways, for example:

- people who use lots of jargon
- people who use lots of slang
- people who swear

Once you have gathered your data you are ready to begin. Your response should include:

- A section explaining how people are regarded because of their language use and why this is so. You should use evidence from your research data.
- Your views on how language use defines our identities.
- A conclusion in which you make a summary of your thoughts, including what you believe other people might think of the way you speak.

> **Remember:** this task is about analysis and explanation. Keep your focus on how to make your reader understand what you want them to know. Like all the assignments in this section, you need to have enough information to write 800–1,000 words.

Student response to Task A

Do you swear? I *!#?*! well do, but not while my mother is around. Why? Because I value my life. Also, she has an image of me as the personification of perfection. This is a perspective I would not like to diminish. It makes my mother feel better. Help the Aged? Possibly.

I didn't think I modified my language to suit different audiences but obviously I do. It seems that this is because I play the role that they expect of me. My family sees and hears one side of me. My friends see quite another. My research uncovered startling revelations that indicate I'm not the only one who uses different language in different situations. Are you another?

Examiner's comment

The candidate has linked the task to the real world by looking at spoken language outside of the classroom setting. There is a very personal voice throughout the piece, which is peppered with humour. The opening cleverly brings out the personality of the writer and links it directly to language use. Readers are drawn into the assignment by the rhetorical questions that make them consider their own reactions to the subject. By using the phrase 'My research uncovered startling revelations', the candidate is deliberately choosing language that will create interest in readers and make them want to know what the revelations are. This maintains attention and paves the way for a logical sequence of explanations.

The candidate has achieved all of the necessary requirements for a Grade A.

How to improve

To achieve a Grade A*, the candidate should use the remainder of the assessment to analyse the topic in detail, giving supporting evidence, and explore how our identities are shaped by the language we use.

Assessment for learning

When you are researching, make sure you get your friends to explain their thoughts. This will give you detailed evidence to include in your response and will make it sound more authoritative.

> **Remember:** you need to make your response individual, even though you may have shared some aspects of your research with your friends. This means that you must tell your reader what *you* think.

Spoken genres

Task B

Show how persuasive language is used in real-life situations.

First, copy and complete the table below to record your findings. Use your existing knowledge to complete the first three columns and then analyse your data in the final column.

> **Remember:** persuasive language is used to make you want to do something. It doesn't just happen in advertisements. The work you have done on writing to persuade will help you here.

Place	Reasons persuasive language is used	Who uses persuasive language	Examples of persuasive language	Effect of the persuasive language
Home				
School				
In the media				
Elsewhere				

Assessment for learning

Make sure you give explanations. Ask your friends how clearly you have explained and what parts are not clear.

Student response to Task B

Opening

'Would you like to feel really good? Try one of these.' Intriguing, isn't it? You are already wondering what you are being offered. You're probably feeling tempted. Now try it the other way round. 'Would you like to feel awful? Try one of these.' Are you still enticed by the offer? Of course not. Why? It's doesn't matter what's on offer, it's how the proposal is made that affects your choice — the language that is used. I don't want to buy a three-piece suite, but there are plenty of people on television with the power to persuade me that I do.

It's not just on television. I'm immersed in persuasive language at home, at school and everywhere I go. I'm convinced I need products to reduce my cholesterol. I don't even know what cholesterol is! I go to bed early because my mother tells me that every hour before midnight is worth two afterwards. I use Lynx because it will make me irresistible to women. All of this because I am easily susceptible to persuasive language.

WOULD YOU LIKE TO FEEL REALLY GOOD?

TRY ONE OF THESE

YOU'RE IRRESISTIBLE

Examiner's comment

The candidate has approached the response in a very individual way. You are in no doubt that the views expressed are the candidate's own. However, they are delivered in such a way that the reader can relate to them. The use of rhetorical questions pushes the reader into agreeing with the candidate's feelings. The style of the response is witty and satirical, using humour and irony to create an effect. This candidate has achieved all of the necessary requirements for a Grade A.

However, the task is about explaining the effect of persuasive language. This answer has concentrated on the candidate's response and has not given any specific examples or analysis. In order to achieve a Grade A*, the candidate now needs to focus on how persuasive language is used in different situations and places. It is important that the candidate uses evidence from other people to illustrate the points that are being made.

Assessment for learning

Discuss your draft ideas with some friends. Ask them whether you have got the balance right between opinions, evidence and analysis, and where you need to make changes.

Multi-modal task

Task C

Research and explain how Shakespeare could use new technologies in *Macbeth*.
Before you begin, talk to your friends about social networking sites. Make sure you discuss the language that is used in electronic communication. How is it different to speech, and why? If you have never used a social networking site, ask someone who has to explain to you how they work.

Remember: this assessment is about explaining and exploring your ideas. The work you have done on writing to explain and inform will help you here.

Student response to Task C

'New technology' and 'Shakespeare'. The words hardly belong in the same sentence, but I'm told he was far in advance of his time so I think he would have embraced new technologies enthusiastically and used them to the full. Just think of the innovations he could have used. Macbeth would probably have got away with it!

Let's start at the beginning with the Witches. 'When shall we three meet again?' Nowadays that would be easy to work out on Facebook. They could even be having a multi-point video-conference, like I do with my friends. Their assignations with Macbeth could easily be done by a conference call.

Apple

What about Duncan's murder? Easy. Lady Macbeth could ring the guard's mobile phones to check they were asleep. Let's face it, everyone answers their phone! She could text Macbeth to see what he was doing. He could reply with a video-phone message so she could actually see the dead body. Both of them could watch up-to-the-minute reports on the internet to follow the murder enquiry.

Would MacDuff need to go to London to see Malcolm? Absolutely not! A simple e-mail would have done the job. MacDuff could have stayed in Fife and the 'little chickens' would not have been goosed!

Shakespeare was at the forefront of invention, so I think he would have loved modern technology. I wonder if the battle scene at the end could have been done on an X-Box with enhanced computer graphics.

Examiner's comment

The candidate's confident introduction links Shakespeare to new technologies and makes it clear how they could be used. There are clear 'before' and 'after' sections, which show the effect on the candidate. This is an original and personal response, which expresses the candidate's thoughts clearly and offers thorough explanations. There is obvious wit and humour. This response would achieve a Grade A.

How to improve

To achieve a Grade A*, the candidate needs to analyse and evaluate the effects of new technologies. This means that he/she should explain in detail how they would be used and how they would enhance a performance.

Remember: the key to all of the assignments relating to AO2 is to make sure you do some research. Without it, you won't be able to offer any explanations. Although you are focusing on your spoken language skills, your research will need you to call on your reading and writing skills too.

C

Writing

Chapter 7

Assessment Objectives for writing

Writing makes up 40% of the marks for GCSE English. It is an important skill, because being able to write well for different purposes helps in many situations in our daily lives. Writing can be divided into two types: non-fiction texts and creative texts. Your skills in creating and writing 'believable' responses in your written pieces of work or answers will be assessed. As a writer of high calibre, you have to ensure your work stands out from the crowd. Has it got the X-factor?

Your writing in English Language will be assessed against the following Assessment Objectives. Please note that AO4 in the English Language specification is the same as AO3 in the English specification. To avoid confusion, this textbook refers to the AO as AO3.

AO3(i)	**Communicate clearly** and **imaginatively**, **using**, **adapting** and **selecting vocabulary** appropriate to task and purpose in ways that engage the reader.
AO3(ii)	**Organise** information and ideas into **structured and sequenced** sentences, paragraphs and whole texts, using a variety of **linguistic structural features** to support **cohesion** and overall **coherence**.
AO3(iii)	Use a range of **sentence structures** for **clarity, purpose** and **effect** with **accurate punctuation and spelling**.

AO3(i)

Communicate clearly and imaginatively, using, adapting and selecting vocabulary appropriate to task and purpose in ways that engage the reader

Key words	What the key words mean for A* students
communicate clearly	You express your ideas with great clarity so it impacts on the reader.
imaginatively	Your use of imagination is immersed impressively in your chosen genre.
adapting and selecting vocabulary	Your vocabulary choices are 'delightful', show sophistication and are suited impressively to audience and purpose.

AO3(ii)

Organise information and ideas into structured and sequenced sentences, paragraphs and whole texts, using a variety of linguistic structural features to support cohesion and overall coherence

Key words	What the key words mean for A* students
organise information and ideas	All parts of your text fit well together and form a united whole. Key features are embedded skillfully throughout exuding sophistication.
structured and sequenced	Paragraphs and other structural and organisational devices, such as discourse markers, fully complement the style, audience and purpose of the piece.
variety of linguistic structural features	The way you use language leaves a lasting impact on the reader.
cohesion and overall coherence	Your text is strongly coherent throughout and makes an impact as a whole. This means it is well-planned, clear and sensible, with all the parts complementing each other and going well together.

Remember: cohesion and coherence are key elements of A* writing.

AO3(iii)

Use a range of sentence structures for clarity, purpose and effect with accurate punctuation and spelling

Key words	What the key words mean for A* students
range of sentence structures	Sophisticated and varied types of sentences, creating impressive effects.
clarity, purpose and effect	Your writing is clear and matches the purpose for which it is written and in doing so has a powerful effect on the reader.
accurate punctuation and spelling	Your spelling shows remarkable control. Your use of punctuation shows you can use a range of punctuation accurately to make an impact on the reader.

Remember: clarity, purposefulness and accuracy are key characteristics of A* writing.

Where is AO3 assessed?

AO3 is assessed just about everywhere you are assessed for writing. It tests whether you can write well and make clear links between your writing and the intended style, audience and purpose (SAP). You will be assessed for writing in Unit 1 and Unit 3; both units have an equal weighting of 20%, making up a total of 40%.

How is AO3(iii) assessed?

This AO is assessed through controlled assessment and external examination. Both forms of assessment require the same skills for writing.

Reading questions

You will need to read questions carefully and interpret what they are actually asking you to do. One good way of doing this is to underline the key words in the question.

Make every word count

To achieve a Grade A*, you need to ensure that every word, sentence and paragraph is impressive. You should show an awareness of style, form, audience and purpose, and immerse yourself in the genre you are tackling. If you can do so, your writing will display sophistication.

Examiners and mark schemes frequently refer to A* writing as being 'delightful' and showing 'flair' and 'originality'. 'Delightful' means giving pleasure to the reader; 'flair' means showing a natural talent or aptitude (skill); and 'originality' means showing independent thought and writing in a way that is new, inventive and well-crafted in continuous prose (written in full sentences which flow well).

Remember: sophistication and flair are key characteristics of A* work.

What you write should be 'compelling,' (this means it is forceful and interesting), and 'convincing,' (believable and as realistic as the purpose demands).

Skills to achieve a Grade A/A*

In summary, to gain a Grade A/A*, you will need to demonstrate:
- clarity in your communication
- craft (well-structured writing)
- coherence
- continuous prose
- compelling content
- convincing texts
- complexity (of grammatical structures and punctuation)

Integrated writing skills

This section will help you develop the A* skills needed for each part of AO3. Remember, though, that all three parts of AO3 are examined at the same time in your writing. The tasks focus on one key element, but you will ultimately have to integrate all the aspects of AO3.

Task A

Describe a sinister world.

The question doesn't specify where or what this world is, so it is up to you to interpret it in a sophisticated way to grab the reader's attention. What will make your response stand out and be different?

Always plan before you start as it allows you to order your thoughts. List your ideas and then number them to create a coherent structure.

Student response to Task A

Plan

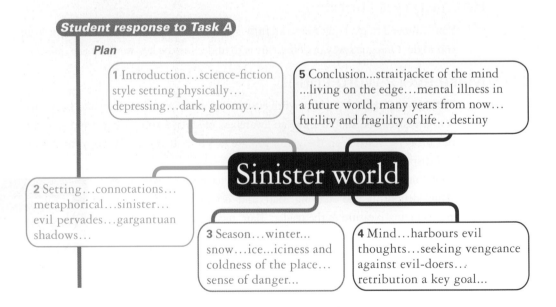

1 Introduction...science-fiction style setting physically... depressing...dark, gloomy...

5 Conclusion...straitjacket of the mind ...living on the edge...mental illness in a future world, many years from now... futility and fragility of life...destiny

Sinister world

2 Setting...connotations... metaphorical...sinister... evil pervades...gargantuan shadows...

3 Season...winter... snow...ice...iciness and coldness of the place... sense of danger...

4 Mind...harbours evil thoughts...seeking vengeance against evil-doers... retribution a key goal...

Darkness and gloom began to descend as the twilight curtain slowly fell. The once imperturbable aura that existed many moons ago was now unimaginable. Depression and dejection enveloped every angle, every curve of this ferocious land.

Gargantuan shadows loomed like malnourished predators eager to consume whatever, whosoever, may venture into their sparsely trodden path. Sinister evil pervades this forgotten world. Sinister parasites stand triumphant where once virginal thoughts lay. Life was no longer sacred; peace was no longer a destiny. Sons had slain their mothers, the very sources of their life, leaving them discarded like abandoned umbilical cords, their purpose fulfilled. Daughters of Eden wept and wailed, lamenting the loss of innocence.

Glaciers frozen in their majesty riveted my thoughts for a while. I knew not where I was. No one knew where I was. Acres of ice seasoned the land; spectres protruding in unwanted dreams. There was nowhere to hide; no one to hide with.

Here I was, the fortuitous combination of circumstances, harbouring evil. Seeking vengeance; seeking retribution. Solace truanted from this unwelcome world. Unfamiliar relentless forces I could not comprehend searched for peace and solitude.

Studio-54/Fotolia

Cruel concepts, the futility and fragility of life in this barren universe, reign victorious. Yet this was my utopia; my destiny. I struggled unashamedly with my thoughts; my conquerors. Freedom seemed to be a distant land and the beating drums reverberated mercilessly, leaving me helpless like regurgitated remnants strewn across a wasteland. My breathing accelerated as yet another stranger's voice resonated, senseless and unmerciful. She tightened the rough leather straps of the clinically ice-white jacket, pulling my arms firmly behind me. I was transfixed, conscious yet unconscious; aware yet unaware. In her gaze, a fluttering reflection revealed deeply saddened eyes protruding from a weary face; she could not see into the straitjacket of my mind and the unspoken despondency that lay there in the realms of a sinister world she could not even begin to comprehend…

Examiner's comment

This candidate has written a well-communicated response that is both convincing and compelling. He/she has imaginatively interpreted the sinister world as someone's struggle with mental illness — a physical and mental straightjacket. There are suggestions at the end of the response that the narrator may be a patient in a mental hospital. The reader is totally immersed in the world before this revelation. The image of this world is further enhanced by the idea that the response is set in a futuristic world. The candidate's vocabulary choices are delightful and the whole text shows sophistication. This response fulfills the criteria for a Grade A*.

Photooiasson/Fotolia

Assessment for learning

Identify the types of punctuation used in the student's response. Are there instances where different punctuation could be used to widen the range? Use a thesaurus to look up key words and see if you can find alternatives. Learn any that you are unfamiliar with — as an A* candidate, you should constantly be widening your vocabulary.

Writing

Chapter 8

Writing for real-life contexts

Writing for real-life contexts appears in Unit 1. It is assessed through a 1-hour exam and makes up 20% of the marks available for your English/English language GCSE. Another term for this style of writing is 'non-fiction'.

There are many situations in real life where you will have to write texts that can explain, argue or advise. You need to be able to write texts in a way that is acceptable to others in order for your views to be heard. This skill can be described as 'making realistic representations', or to put it simply, responding to what could potentially be real-life situations.

To be a successful writer, you need to understand **style**, **audience** and **purpose** (SAP). This chapter looks at different forms of writing, probable audiences, a selection of purposes for writing, and a range of styles. All of these elements are interlinked. You need to craft your writing carefully to include them, so that you can gain the best possible mark.

AO3

The Assessment Objectives for the controlled writing assessment (Unit 3) and the external examination (Unit 1) are exactly the same. Your writing will be assessed against AO3. The key words are emboldened in the table overleaf. They are explained in Chapter 7, pages 60–61.

AO3(i)	**Communicate clearly** and **imaginatively**, **using**, **adapting** and **selecting vocabulary** appropriate to task and purpose in ways that engage the reader.
AO3(ii)	**Organise** information and ideas into **structured and sequenced** sentences, paragraphs and whole texts, using a variety of **linguistic structural features** to support **cohesion** and overall **coherence**.
AO3(iii)	Use a range of **sentence structures** for **clarity, purpose** and **effect** with **accurate punctuation and spelling**.

Note that at least one third of the marks will be allocated to AO3(iii).

Where is AO3 assessed?

In Unit 1, AO3 is assessed in Section B of the examination paper. As is the case in Unit 3, AO3 tests whether you can write well and with clarity, and use SAP successfully. Unit 1 is common to both GCSE English and GCSE English Language.

The exam

In the Higher Tier exam paper, you will be asked to complete two compulsory writing tasks:

- one short writing task (SWT), worth 16 marks
- one long writing task (LWT), worth 24 marks

Together they make up a total of 40 marks. All three parts of AO3 will be tested in each question. Although the same AOs are tested in both papers, their weighting is slightly different, as shown in the table:

Assessment Objective (AO)	SWT – marks allocated for an A*/16	LWT – marks allocated for an A*/24
AO3(i) and AO3(ii)	8–10	13–16
AO3(iii)	5–6	6–8

You will be asked to write in a range of genres, adapting your style to fit the real-life situation for which you are writing.

The short task (16 marks)

The 16 marks available are divided as follows:

- 10 marks for communication and organisation
- 6 marks for using a range of sentence structures and writing accurately

Criteria for a Grade A/A*

To gain an A*, you need to show evidence of the following criteria:

Communication	Your writing, interpretation and communication of the task is 'convincing and compelling'. Your writing is engaging and your ideas are detailed and developed, and sometimes abstract. The tone is appropriate and effective. You evoke a response from the reader. Your use of linguistic devices such as rhetoric and hyperbole is effective. Discourse markers are extensive and controlled.
Organisation	You write the whole of the text in continuous prose and your paragraphs enhance meaning. Structural features are used appropriately and effectively. Complex ideas are presented coherently.
Range of sentence structures	You use a variety of sentence structures: simple, compound and complex.
Writing accurately	Overall, your spelling, punctuation, grammar, sentence structure, paragraphing etc. are accurate and 'all in the correct place'.

Task A

Write a letter to a friend explaining why you would like him or her to accompany you on a family trip abroad.

> **Remember:** all three parts of AO3 are all being tested — communication, organisation, sentence structure, punctuation and spelling.

Student response to Task A

Plan

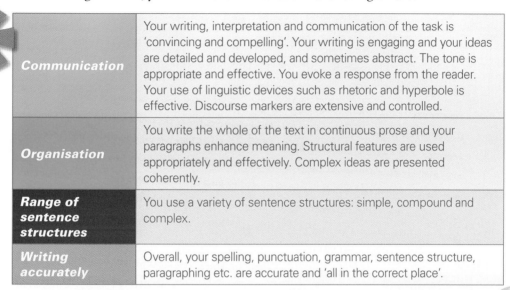

> **Remember:** you must use a range of sentences in your work — simple, compound and complex.

Answer

12 Old Lane

Cumbria

CB1 2VM

Dear Kamran,

I am so excited to be able to invite you to join us on a fabulous holiday. It was unbelievable when we perused the holiday brochures to see the white sandy beaches in Morocco. They were so enticing and I could almost inhale the invigorating air from the sapphire-blue sea, smell the freshness of pollution-free air! My family has never planned such an exotic and luxurious holiday and it will be made even more enjoyable by having you there with me to share the experience. We will be going on 1st August and returning on the 14th — fourteen days of sheer luxury that are unimaginable during the hectic school term!

Oleg Deleznev/Fotolia

Marrakech is a magical place. The hotel we will be staying in is Les Deux Tours, which is located in the heart of the Palmeraie region and about a 20-minute drive from Marrakech. We will travel in a hotel shuttle-bus along a narrow, dusty track paved with a seemingly interminable expanse of deep, emerald-green palm trees, which my mum says resembles an almost biblical setting. The landscape is sprinkled with small hamlets and houses that seem extraordinarily misplaced compared to the opulence and splendour of Les Deux Tours. Two majestic towers overlook the main entrance, beckoning its guests into a land of mystery and intrigue. We will be living like kings and ancient pharaohs — well, at least for two weeks!

The hotel has its own private villas, one of which will be ours for the duration of our stay. Our villa is enclosed within its own private walled gardens, a sensational swimming pool, and a full-size games room with a professional snooker table and dartboard. There is a 52-inch plasma TV screen connected to a Wii — how amazing is that? We will not be able to resist a visit to the world-famous hammams, or Turkish baths. You know how baths are normally relaxing? Well, I believe this kind of bath is a little more energising and will certainly invigorate us.

The exotic lifestyle will certainly be an entirely new experience for us both — a welcome change from tranquil Cumbria. There is a range of activities available to us, including a camel trek that pass through Kasbahs and oases, then stops at the sand dunes at Nekla. We can stay in a real Berber tent and eat tantalising tagines for dinner. Meeting and staying among the locals will be an unforgettable experience. Their poverty is no barrier to their hospitality and their appreciation of life — this is what my father tells me, as he has been before. I am told that we will leave appreciating the opportunities and abundance of wealth we have in the West.

I think this holiday will be amazing for us both. Please say yes to sharing this fantastic and potentially life-changing experience with us.

Hope to hear from you soon,

Troy

Serge di Marco/Fotolia

Examiner's comment

This candidate has written a well-communicated response, which is convincingly conveyed. It shows clarity of thought, and the detailed ideas engage the reader.

Form, style, audience and purpose are sustained throughout. Linguistic devices are used effectively and discourse markers are well-controlled. The piece is well-organised, with paragraphs enhancing meaning — this means the beginning of each paragraph helps to put your point across powerfully; while the rest of the paragraph expands on that point and makes the reader think about or 'hear' what you say. This candidate fulfills the A* grade criteria.

Assessment for learning

Identify the different types of sentence structures the candidate has used to answer Task A. Are they simple, compound or complex? Can you improve any of them? Copy and complete the table below, using examples from the student response plus sentences of your own.

Type of sentence	Example from student response to Task A	My own example
Simple		
Compound		
Complex		

Writing

Chapter 9

Punctuation

Punctuation is a key part of AO3. Remember, AO3(iii) asks for 'accurate punctuation'. Punctuation enhances meaning, and using it accurately will give credibility and conviction to what you say. Your writing will therefore have more impact on your intended audience, and of course gain you more marks too.

It isn't possible to grasp accurate punctuation by referring quickly to a textbook. Instead, you need to practice in every piece of written work you do. Make a conscious effort to improve and develop your handling of a range of punctuation, so you can add impact and clarity to your texts. A* students use punctuation successfully throughout their work.

Key words	What the key words mean
accurate punctuation	Full stops and commas must be used accurately. You should know how putting a comma in a certain place helps to make meaning clear and can even enhance meaning. Accurate punctuation also includes the appropriate use of inverted commas for speech marks and quotations, and exclamation marks and question marks. The confident Grade C and above student will also know how to use apostrophes, colons and semi-colons. A* students will show flair and precision in doing so.

Task A

Photocopy the following article from the *Guardian* newspaper. Then put in the appropriate capital letters and punctuation.

The catholic Church and euthanasia

Its popularly believed that Catholics are anti euthanasia. Do Catholics believe we dont have the freedom to do as we like?

St Thomas More who was canonised by Pope Pius XI in 1935 claimed in *Utopia* that euthanasia for the terminally ill was a central factor needed in the ideal society

Horticulture/Fotolia

when any is taken with a torturing and lingering pain so that there is no hope either of recovery or ease the priests and magistrates come and exhort them, that since they are now unable to go on with the business of life and are become a burden to themselves and to all about them so that they have really outlived themselves they would no longer nourish such a rooted distemper but would choose rather to die since they cannot live but in much misery being assured that if they either deliver themselves from their prison and torture or are willing that others should do it they shall be happy after their deaths Such as are wrought on by these persuasions, do either starve themselves of their own accord, or they take opium, and so they die without pain but no man is forced on this way of ending his life and if they cannot be persuaded to it they do not for that fail in their attendance and care of them

How times change in 1980 the catholic church proclaimed the 'declaration on euthanasia' which states that Intentionally causing ones own death or suicide is... equally as wrong as murder and that no one can in any way permit the killing of an innocent human being, whether a foetus or an embryo, an infant or an adult, an old person, or one suffering from an incurable disease, or a person who is dying...

What about the situation where doctors are asked for drugs, whose main purpose is to bring about death What are Catholics to make of this

Heather McDougall

Assessment for learning

Assess your own work by checking your use of punctuation against the original article. You can find it at:

www.guardian.co.uk/commentisfree/belief/2009/aug/27/religion-catholicism

Sentence structure, punctuation and spelling (SSPS) for AO3	
Grade A/A*	• Punctuation and grammar is used with success. • Writing is organised, with sentences clearly demarcated. • A variety of sentence forms are used to good effect. • Ambitious vocabulary is used and spelt correctly. • Standard English is used appropriately.

Task B

Write a magazine article that argues the case for or against legalising euthanasia in the UK. You should aim it at adults. As well as the content of your answer, you should focus on your use of punctuation. Choose a range of punctuation that is highly effective and well-selected. Refer to the table above to ensure you meet the A* criteria.

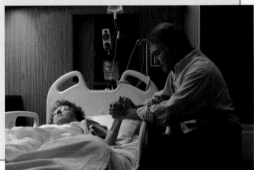

Claudio's Pics/Fotolia

Student response to Task B

There is something quite haunting about removing treatment from people who are dying, especially when carried out by those who have taken an oath to protect life and the very sanctity of it! There are some perverted views in the public domain that tirelessly advocate that it is somehow compassionate to actively give assistance to someone who is terminally ill to end their life. Surely it is more important to ensure that the cycle of life is allowed to permeate human life, as it does the world of nature? We are all meant to live and eventually die and whether or not there is any human intervention is irrelevant. Life must come and life must go. Que sera sera?

Doctors and families already make very difficult decisions, such as switching off life-support systems, DNR (Do Not Resuscitate), and in a sense these are already a form of euthanasia. Is there any need for further laws legalising assisted suicide? Where then do the boundaries lie? In approximately one third of all deaths, 170,000 doctors withdrew drugs or treatment, hastening the deaths of patients (www.spiked-online.com). This is far more significant than the 3,000 assisted suicide deaths. The media frenzy to legalise this seems a little worn. There are opportunities for patients, their families and doctors to decide at which point further treatment would not be beneficial or prolong life. Surely a patient who is daunted by a potentially terminal illness no longer has the full and free mental capacity to choose to live or die, as this decision will inevitably be tainted by the traumas envisaged by the patient? Life, surely, should be allowed to take its own course; there have been people who have recovered against seemingly insurmountable odds.

On the other hand, one could also argue that health authorities propagate postcode lotteries and play God by withdrawing drugs for the treatment of cancer simply because they are expensive. Can we put a cost on human life? Is it society's place to do so?

Examiner's comment

This A* student has approached the topic seriously and diligently. He/she has used a range of punctuation, such as a semi-colons, brackets, hyphens and question marks. The writing is clearly organised and includes a variety of simple, compound and complex sentences. The student has used statistics to make the argument more convincing and to have more impact on the reader. Discourse markers are used accurately and the paragraphs are well-structured.

Remember: in an exam, where you don't have access to statistics to support a given argument, you can make them up. Try not to be too random! Think carefully about the statistic you are giving so it can support your argument effectively.

Assessment for learning

Try to further develop and sustain the student's response to Task B. Make sure you match its tone and style, and that you meet all of the criteria for Grades A/A*.

C

Writing

Chapter 10

Writing formats

To succeed in Section B of the examination, especially on Paper 1, you need to know the key writing formats. You can consider these formats to be the formulas or frameworks within which you write. For example, if you are asked to write a letter, you need know what elements make a good and successful letter.

This chapter will take you through some of the key writing formats, so that you can learn them, practice them and apply what you have learned to the tasks in the examination — and indeed, in any situation in your life where you have to write. Writing non-fiction successfully is an important functional life skill.

You can probably easily think of the times when you will have to write a letter, but you may be less sure as to why you need to learn how to write an article or review. If you understand how articles and reviews are created, their purpose, how to interpret them and how to identify their bias elements, you will be able to reach your own conclusions about what you see and hear on the news and read in newspapers and magazines. You will even be able to interpret images and texts you see around you, such as posters and adverts.

The key words for AO3 are emboldened in the table below. They are explained in Chapter 7, pages 60–61.

AO3(i)	**Communicate clearly** and **imaginatively**, **using**, **adapting** and **selecting vocabulary** appropriate to task and purpose in ways that engage the reader.
AO3(ii)	**Organise** information and ideas into **structured and sequenced** sentences, paragraphs and whole texts, using a variety of **linguistic structural features** to support **cohesion** and overall **coherence**.
AO3(iii)	Use a range of **sentence structures** for **clarity, purpose** and **effect** with **accurate punctuation and spelling**.

Where is AO3 assessed?

AO3 is assessed just about everywhere you are assessed for writing, in both English and in English Language.

How is AO3 assessed?

AO3 is assessed in both the English and English Language GCSE courses. It is assessed in Unit 1: understanding and producing non-fiction texts and in Section B of the written examinations, through two compulsory writing tasks — a short writing task and a long writing task. The names of the triplets you may have become accustomed to at Key Stage 3 are not necessarily provided on the examination paper, but it is useful to know what they are:

- discuss, argue, persuade
- inform, explain, describe

The examiner will expect you to be able to use these well. This is especially the case when writing non-fiction texts.

AO3 is also assessed in Unit 3 in the controlled assessments, in the form of creative writing tasks. In English, the creative writing task is worth a total of 40 marks; in English Language, it is worth a total of 30 marks.

> *Remember:* competent Grade A/A* writers show confidence and assured control over what they write. They are able to craft their writing, manipulating the content and the impact it has on their intended audience.

Criteria for a Grade A/A*

Below are the general criteria for writing for Grades A/A*. You should aim to meet them in all your writing.

Communication and organisation	Shows a confident and assured control over a range of forms and styles appropriate to different tasks and purposes. Texts written are engaging and hold the reader's interest throughout through logical arguments, persuasive force or creative delight.
Linguistic and structural features	These are skilfully used to sequence texts and achieve coherence. A wide range of sentence structure is used, ensuring clarity. Vocabulary choices, punctuation and spelling are ambitious, imaginative and correct.

Writing formats

We all experience different writing formats in our everyday life: a charity leaflet through the door, a newspaper or magazine we buy, reviews for a film we want to see at the cinema, and so on. GCSE English and English Language require that you can recognise and write in different key formats.

It is a good idea to collect real-life examples of the writing formats you come across, and to practise highlighting and labelling their features. Try to learn the features of each writing format and practise listing them. Develop your skills by creating examples of writing formats and answering your own tasks on those formats you are least confident in tackling. Think like a teacher!

This chapter describes the key features of the following writing formats:

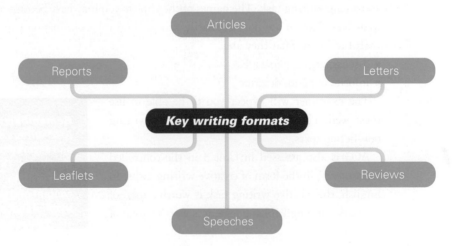

You will be given opportunities to use these features in your own writing. The features list is not wholly exhaustive, and some of the writing formats are addressed in more detail than others. Your teacher may point out additional writing formats to you.

Reports

Headings

Appropriate audience

Clarity

Appropriate tone

Information

Organisation: introduction, conclusion, recommendations

Task A

Find examples of reports on the internet about interesting or controversial topics, such as standards in care homes, abortion, schools or animal testing. Print a report that interests you and use the list above to highlight the key features.

Remember: you write reports about your science experiments. Look at one of these and identify the key features of a report.

Task B

Choose a controversial topic. Using one of the reports you found on the internet as a style model, write your own report on the topic. An example of a suitable topic is the use of body scanners in airports.

Remember: it is good practice to read up on controversial topics often referred to in the news. This will broaden your knowledge of subject areas and enhance your writing. You will become more aware of the issues related to important topics and adopt a mature and sophisticated approach in your examination answers.

Articles

Caption

Catchy title, often with a pun (play on words)

Clear first paragraph

Three or four content paragraphs

Photograph related to the article (do not draw, write a one-line description in the space)

Charts, diagrams etc. (indicate where these would go, but do not draw)

Short and clear summary

Task C

Below is the first part of an article on global warming from the *New York Times*. Photocopy the extract or read it in full on the internet. As you read it through, highlight and label the key features of an article.

Global warming

By Andrew C. Revkin

Jan Will/Fotolia

Overview

Global warming has become perhaps the most complicated issue facing world leaders. On the one hand, warnings from the scientific community are becoming louder, as an increasing body of science points to rising dangers from the ongoing build-up of human-related greenhouse gases — produced mainly by the burning of fossil fuels and forests. On the other, the technological, economic and political issues that have to be resolved before a concerted worldwide effort to reduce emissions can begin have gotten no simpler, particularly in the face of a global economic slowdown.

After years of preparation for climate talks taking place in Copenhagen through 18 December 2009, President Obama and other leaders announced on 15 November what had already become evident — that no formal treaty could be produced anytime soon. Instead, the leaders pledged to reach a placeholder accord that would call for reductions in emissions and increased aid to help developing nations adapt to a changing climate and get access to non-polluting energy options.

This would in theory give the nations more time to work out the all-important details. Negotiators would then seek a binding global agreement in 2010, complete with firm emission targets, enforcement mechanisms and specific dollar amounts to aid poorer nations.

At the heart of the debate is a momentous tussle between rich and poor countries over who steps up first and who pays most for changed energy menus…

(Read the rest of the article at http://topics.nytimes.com/top/news/science/topics/globalwarming/index.html#)

© New York Times, 8 December 2009

Task D

Now use the key features to write your own article. Use the *New York Times* example above and those you found on the internet. Make sure you refer to the Grade A/A* criteria given in the table on page 76.

Assessment for learning

Label the format features in an article you have written in one colour. Then take another colour and mark the features of A/A* writing. Does your writing fulfil all of the criteria? Redraft your article to add any corrections you need, such as including a range of punctuation.

Letters

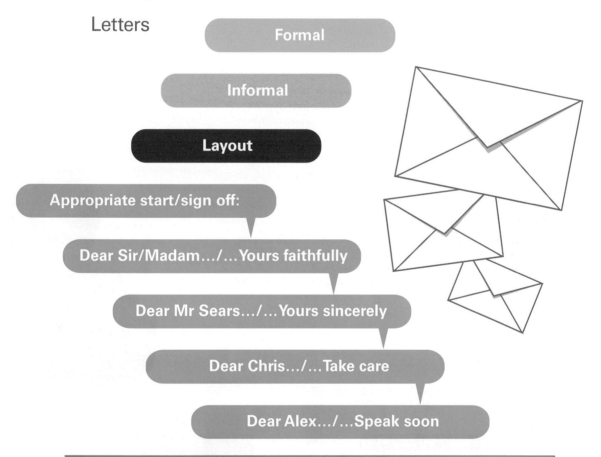

Formal

Informal

Layout

Appropriate start/sign off:

Dear Sir/Madam.../...Yours faithfully

Dear Mr Sears.../...Yours sincerely

Dear Chris.../...Take care

Dear Alex.../...Speak soon

Task E

Read the student response below, a letter from an adult complaining to the council about teenagers causing trouble in the local area. Identify which format features this student has used successfully. Point out and correct those format features the student has not quite managed to develop.

Student's response to Task E

Katie Cartwright
49 Bristol Close
Banks
Birmingham
B22 3JC

Councillor T. Reeves

333 Robin Drive

Banks

Birmingham

B22 5JC

Dear Councillor Reeves

I am writing to express my concerns over the growing levels of anti-social behaviour in my local area. As a resident of Banks for 20 years, I have never known things to be so bad. I feel I am living my life in fear of reprisals from teenagers who are just out of control and out of touch with how people are feeling about their behaviour.

Many members of the local community feel as strongly as I do. A lot of trouble has been caused by teenagers who are joyriding in cars very much under the wrong impression that scaring residents, especially children, is cool. Only last week a child was quite seriously injured as he ran away frightened from one such car, straight into a side street without looking, where another car was speeding past. Extremely frightening! Does something more serious need to happen to make the council do something to stop this? We have complained so many times but no one seems to listen...

I look forward to hearing from you as a matter of urgency.

Yours sincerely

K. Cartwright

(Ms Katie Cartwright)

Assessment for learning

Be the examiner and write a comment on the student's letter. You could start: 'The student has used the required format of writing a formal letter, using formal language. The text itself is interesting...'

Task F

Redraft the letter in Task E into an A* response. Use the advice you were given in Task D and the Grade A/A* criteria in the table on page 76 to help you include the appropriate content.

Task G

Write a letter to the Prime Minister complaining about the lack of availability of drugs to treat all cancer patients.

Student response to Task G

Adam Sellers
38 North Road
Peckham
London
SE33 5EN

The Prime Minister
10 Downing Street
London
SW1A 2AA

Dear Prime Minister

I am writing to you to inform you of my views on a topic that is not only of national importance but also one of great personal gravity.

Should we face postcode lotteries according to where we live when receiving life-saving treatment for cancer? Prime Minister, it is with regret that many of us find this to be the case. How would you feel if this concerned a member of your family or even your own children?

A few months ago, a great personal tragedy struck my family. I have an aunt living in the West Midlands who has recently had to endure chemotherapy treatment. One cannot emphasise enough how traumatising this process has already been for her, a single mother, and her young family of three children aged 3, 5 and 7 years. My aunt needed a drug called Avastin and has recently been informed by her local health authority that there is to be no further issue of the drug as it is no longer financially viable. We researched the internet for information. To our horror and devastation, we discovered that the West Midlands spent a meagre £46 on Avastin per 100 chemotherapy patients. This is an abominable sum when compared to £8,732 in London and an average of £1,748 for England as a whole. I am certain you will be able to verify the figures from the Department of Health. I ask you, Prime Minister — would you wish your daughter to live in the West Midlands if she needed Avastin? I implore you to reconsider such unfair postcode lotteries. My aunt has had to suffer pain because of where she lives. She has paid taxes all her life and has worked selflessly to support her family.

Information from the *Independent* stated that spending on Herceptin per 100 patients varied from '£31,717 in the East of England to £101,597 in the North East, against an English average of £68,753.' Yet again, the harsh reality of a postcode lottery leaves a bittersweet sensation; bitter if you are denied treatment and sweet if you are allowed to be prescribed the drugs you need. All simply because of where you live! Should families now consider where they live far more seriously after reviewing their medical histories?

I ask that you please review the case of my aunt, who desperately needs Avastin, in light of the information that I have presented above. I wait to hear from you urgently and with great anticipation.

Yours faithfully,

A. Sellers

Adam Sellers

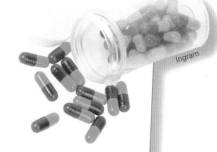
Ingram

Examiner's comment

This candidate communicates in a convincing and compelling way. The topic is not an easy one, and the student evokes empathy and uses statistics to support some serious points on a controversial topic. The letter is formal and sophisticated. There is appropriate use of discourse markers, and linguistic devices such as rhetorical questions are used effectively. It is well organised and written in continuous prose. Complex ideas are presented coherently and the paragraphs enhance meaning effectively (i.e. the beginning of each paragraph helps to put your point across powerfully; while the rest of the paragraph expands on that point and makes the reader think about or 'hear' what you say). This candidate would attain a Grade A*.

Assessment for learning

Plan and write the response you think the candidate might receive from the Prime Minister. Highlight all the A/A* features in your letter, then redraft it, in pairs if possible, to fulfil all the A* criteria. Next you should write an examiner comment, modelling the style of the examiner above.

> **Remember:** planning is essential in structuring your work effectively. Practise using hand plans, tree plans, flow-charts and so on, to help you find the planning tools that work best for you.

Leaflets

Purpose/audience

Heading

Sub-heading

Bullet points

Pictures

Language

Overall impact

You will have had many leaflets posted through your door or given out at school. Collect them and make a list of common and uncommon features. You may even spot some different features to those listed above. Practice creating your own leaflets using ICT, for example Publisher.

Speeches

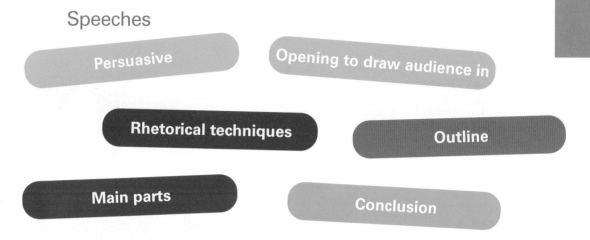

Persuasive

Opening to draw audience in

Rhetorical techniques

Outline

Main parts

Conclusion

Rhetorical devices are vital to writing speeches and other persuasive texts. The following diagram lists many possible rhetorical devices.

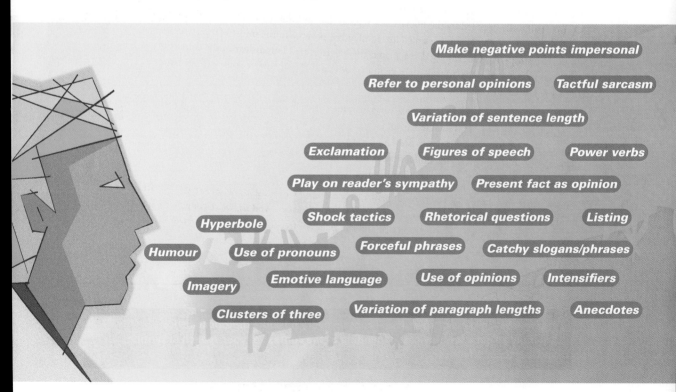

Make negative points impersonal

Refer to personal opinions   Tactful sarcasm

Variation of sentence length

Exclamation   Figures of speech   Power verbs

Play on reader's sympathy   Present fact as opinion

Hyperbole   Shock tactics   Rhetorical questions   Listing

Humour   Use of pronouns   Forceful phrases   Catchy slogans/phrases

Imagery   Emotive language   Use of opinions   Intensifiers

Clusters of three   Variation of paragraph lengths   Anecdotes

Task H

Read this extract from Martin Luther King's 'I Have a Dream' speech. Highlight or underline as many rhetorical devices as you can find. Explain the impact these devices have on their intended audience.

I am happy to join with you today in what will go down in history as the greatest demonstration for freedom in the history of our nation.

Five score years ago, a great American, in whose symbolic shadow we stand today, signed the Emancipation Proclamation. This momentous decree came as a great beacon light of hope to millions of Negro slaves who had been seared in the flames of withering injustice. It came as a joyous daybreak to end the long night of their captivity.

But one hundred years later, the Negro still is not free. One hundred years later, the life of the Negro is still sadly crippled by the manacles of segregation and the chains of discrimination. One hundred years later, the Negro lives on a lonely island of poverty in the midst of a vast ocean of material prosperity. One hundred years later, the Negro is still languished in the corners of American society and finds himself an exile in his own land. And so we've come here today to dramatise a shameful condition...

... This note was a promise that all men, yes, black men as well as white men, would be guaranteed the 'unalienable Rights' of 'Life, Liberty and the pursuit of Happiness.' It is obvious today that America has defaulted on this promissory note, insofar as her citizens of colour are concerned. Instead of honouring this sacred obligation, America has given the Negro people a bad cheque, a cheque which has come back marked 'insufficient funds'.

But we refuse to believe that the bank of justice is bankrupt. We refuse to believe that there are insufficient funds in the great vaults of opportunity of this nation. And so, we've come to cash this cheque, a cheque that will give us upon demand the riches of freedom and the security of justice...

Remember: not every speech will contain every possible rhetorical device. Carefully select a few devices, depending of the context of your speech or writing, and use them effectively.

Task I

Write a speech prohibiting the use of full-body scanners in UK airports.

Student response to Task I

'Life, liberty and the pursuit of happiness' were the ideals people fought for in America, but the words clearly resonate our own belief system here in the United Kingdom and the pride we take in having our civil liberties respected and protected. In these turbulent times, it is our duty and responsibility to stand up for our civil liberties. The government is soon to use full-body scanners at all UK airports, which are said to show nude images of our bodies — all in the name of freedom.

It appears that the 'unalienable rights' our counterparts in America campaigned for, and in substance, we as a nation embrace, are ironically far more alienated than ever before. These body scanners will not serve as deterrents. They will simply encourage would-be terrorists to find other ways of concealing explosives, while causing us, the general public, to allow complete strangers to see nude images of our bodies! How can this be morally right? Notice how there is no debate — such activities are merely introduced in the name of national security, while we are foregoing our civil liberties, which we define by the right to be free and the right to have our privacy respected.

Another reason we should speak up against this measure is because it is invasive, intrusive and could contravene people's right to practise their religion and culture freely. Some religions and cultures, especially in Asia and even devout Christians, promote modesty of the human body. Introducing full-body scanners would be an infringement of their human rights.

Why is there such a focus on air travel? Just as much devastation, if not more, can be caused in busy shopping centres and football stadiums that hold thousands upon thousands of people. Are we going to see full-body scanners being used in all these places too?

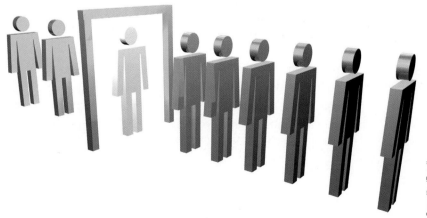

Sogmiller/Fotolia

Already we are the 'most watched' nation in Europe, with our huge number of security cameras. The police can keep our DNA for a period of time even if we are innocent, and we had to go to the European Court of Human Rights to obtain a ruling that they could not retain it indefinitely. Are we now to have our bodies scrutinised at every juncture? One by one, we seem to be sacrificing civil liberty after civil liberty. Is this the kind of world we want our children to inherit?

Examiner's comment

This student shows clarity of thought and provides some succinct arguments. The tone, audience and purpose are clear, and reasons for the prohibition are clearly presented. There is appropriate use of discourse markers. The whole text is written in continuous prose and presents some complex ideas. The answer includes different paragraph lengths. This candidate would attain a Grade A*.

Reviews

Keep the reader's interest

Some detail...but should not give too much away

Often about films, plays, books, shows etc.

Lively, engaging

Task J

Look up reviews of your favourite film on the internet and choose one of them.
- Note the style of the writing.
- Pick out the key features of a review.

Now write a Grade A/A* review of another film in a similar style.

Assessment for learning

Copy out the AO3 A/A* grade criteria below. Tick those you meet. Are there any you still need to work towards?
- write in a compelling way ☐
- engage the reader with detailed, developed ideas ☐
- use a formal, sophisticated tone ☐
- use paragraphs to enhance meaning effectively ☐
- sequence ideas and events coherently ☐
- use a variety of structural features, such as different paragraph lengths ☐
- vary thoughtful, extensive vocabulary choices ☐
- use accurate spelling and a range of punctuation ☐

Finally…

Writing is like any other craft. Master the key skills, and you are well on the way to becoming a skilled, engaging and successful A* writer. You should:

- Familiarise yourself with the different writing forms and formats, and learn the styles required by each. Consider form, audience, purpose and tone, as these are tools that prepare you for writing well.
- Practice writing in different formats using the Grade A* criteria. You should know this well by the time you actually sit the exam.
- Create questions of your own to practice what you have learned. Plan and answer them in timed conditions.
- Discover what your strengths and weaknesses are as a writer, set personal targets and focus on improving these areas in your work, both in the classroom and in work you do at home.

Good luck on your A* journey!